# Good News
# in
# God's Country

# Good News in God's Country

## Adventures of Pioneer Preachers in the Rocky Mountain West

## Steve Lewis

To my loving wife Vicki (Proverbs 31:10) and my father-in-law John M. Claerhout, descendents of pioneer preachers who love the American West.

Design, editing, and production: Steve Lewis
Unless otherwise noted, images are from the author's collection.
Cover photograph courtesy of History Colorado, William Henry Jackson Collection: 20100674.
Chapter inset image: Mount of the Holy Cross, 1873 photograph by William Henry Jackson. Courtesy of United States Geologic Survey Library.

Library of Congress Control Number: 2013950993

ISBN: 978-0-9892807-1-6 (paperback)
       978-0-9892807-2-3 (eBook)

# Preface

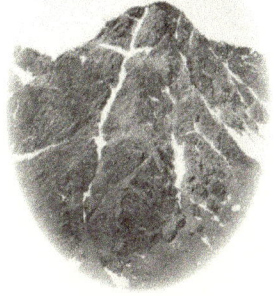

The preachers whose stories are contained in this volume represent a small sample of the hundreds of such ministers who came West to serve the needs of an ever-expanding population. This book tells only a few incidents from the thousands of pages of firsthand accounts contained in the available primary source material. There are many more adventures that should be included here, but some of them were never recorded and are known only to those who experienced them in days long gone.

The inset image is Mount of the Holy Cross in Colorado, which was named for the distinctive cross-shaped snowfield on its northeast slope. The first recorded ascent of Holy Cross was by Dr. F.V. Hayden, photographer W.H. Jackson, and three other men during an 1873 government survey of the area. Holy Cross is one of Colorado's "fourteeners" and among the tallest 100 peaks in the United States. Its image represents the lofty ideals of the home missionary movement as the pioneer preachers explored and ministered in this rugged wilderness.

*Hayden Survey team having a meal in their camp as they prepare for the first recorded ascent of Holy Cross in 1873.*

Courtesy of United States Geologic Survey, photographer William Henry Jackson.

Special thanks are due to the many library archivists across the country who have faithfully preserved the treasures of old manuscripts and photographs over the years. Among their number today are Coi Drummond-Gehrig at Denver Public Library Western History Collection, Melissa VanOtterloo at History Colorado, and Kim Allen Scott at Montana State University Libraries, who have graciously provided materials from their collections.

It is my hope that not only will the stories in this book make for enjoyable reading, but that they would also inspire us to emulate the strength and dedication that characterized these pioneer preachers who helped settle the rugged Rocky Mountain West.

Steve Lewis

# Contents

# Let Them Tell Their
# Stories

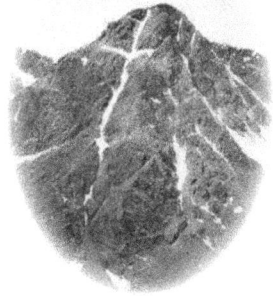

*"How beautiful upon the mountains*
*Are the feet of him who brings good news,*
*Who publishes peace,*
*Who brings good news of happiness,*
*Who publishes salvation."*

Isaiah 52:7

This book is devoted to the stories of pioneer preachers who lived and worked on the frontier in the Rocky Mountain West. Most of their adventures make good reading by themselves, while some require a little background in order to make them even more meaningful. Throughout this book the goal has been to let these remarkable men tell their own stories in their own words.

Few of these preachers would be recognized or remembered today. Some Coloradoans may know of John Lewis Dyer, whose stained glass portrait appears in the dome of the State Capitol building. Some New Mexicans may know the names of Thomas and Emily Harwood, whose Harwood School still exists as a community art center in Albuquerque. Some Montanans may have heard of William Wesley Van Orsdel, who was memorialized in Charles Russell's painting "Brother Van Shooting Buffalo" owned by the Montana Deaconess Medical Center in Great Falls. For the most part, though, these pioneering ministers are long-forgotten. Former University of Colorado professor, the late John B. Schoolland, stated this poignantly in the preface to his history of the

1

*Charles M. Russell painting, "Brother Van Shooting Buffalo," 1909.*
*Inscription: "To Brother Van, from his friend C.M. Russell"*
Courtesy of Great Falls Tribune, File photo used by permission.

First Presbyterian Church in Boulder:

> As one views the record, a kaleidoscope of colorful, devoted men
> and women appear upon the scene, render varied meaningful ser-
> vice, and then gently recede into the shadows. Many once prominent
> and influential names have lost nearly all meaning, but they seem to
> quicken as their deeds are reviewed and contemplated.

In general, the popular histories concerning the American West have
not given much space to the important role of pioneering preachers in
the settlement of this land. Ferenc Szasz, the late professor of history at
the University of New Mexico, expressed this well:

> By ignoring the role of the Protestant clergy, the standard accounts of
> western life have been genuinely remiss. They have neglected a piv-
> otal figure of the trans-Mississippi West. The pioneer clergy devoted
> countless hours to the needs of their own congregations. Moreover,
> their concerns did not simply end at the church door. Instead, they
> performed a variety of far-reaching social roles. Not only did they de-
> liver general public sermons, they also served as librarians, counsel-
> ors, social workers, educators, book sellers, peacekeepers, reformers,
> and general purveyors of culture...In short, the Protestant clergy and

2

their churches proved an integral part of everyday life in the Great Plains and Rocky Mountain West. Their story is worth telling.

One of the goals of this book is to bring back into the light some of the exciting stories from the lives of ministers who have receded into the shadows and been forgotten. Dr. Szasz was right—their stories *are* worth telling! Their adventures make for exciting and inspirational reading. It is the author's hope that readers will be encouraged to become the kind of men and women they were, and to imitate their self-sacrifice and determination to do good in today's world.

# They Lived in Interesting Times

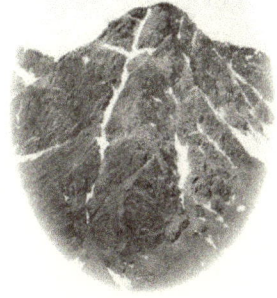

To set the stage for the stories that follow, it helps to understand the times and events which launched the movement of pioneer preachers into the western region of the nation. At the time the United States won its freedom from Great Britain, the population of the country was clustered along the Atlantic coast from Maine to Georgia. The rest of America as we know it today was divided about equally between France and Spain, known to them as the Province of Louisiana and New Spain. But that was soon to change.

After the Revolutionary War in April 1782, peace negotiations began at the Hotel d'York in Paris. John Adams, Benjamin Franklin, John Jay, and Henry Laurens represented the United States, and Franklin wanted the British to cede most of eastern Canada to the United States. He believed that further conflict was inevitable if Britain shared a physical border with America. The British refused to cede eastern Canada, but they did grant more than 250,000 square miles of land northwest of the Ohio River. This area became known as the Northwest Territory, and plans were immediately set in motion to survey, settle, and govern the new territory.

This was the first large tract to be added to the United States, and several important pieces of legislation were enacted to provide for its incorporation into the new nation. Some have said that, apart from the Declaration of Independence and the Constitution of the United States, the Northwest Ordinance of 1787 was the most significant

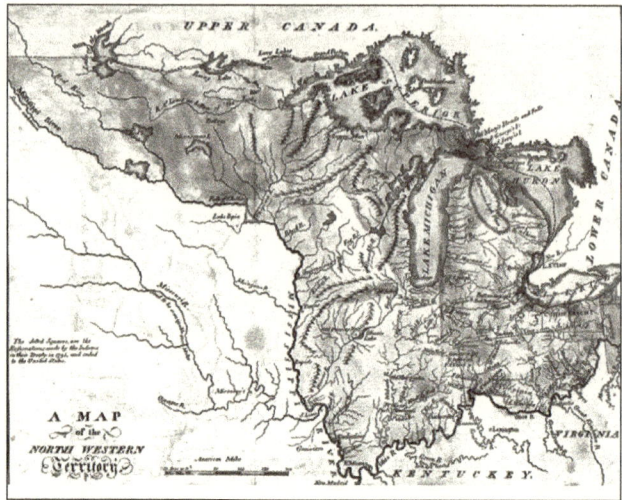

*Early US government map of the Northwest Territory.*

Courtesy of Library of Congress Prints and Photographs Division.

and far-reaching document in the nation's history. Its principles would dictate the handling of territorial expansion for more than a century to come, and it would ensure that each newly formed territory could eventually achieve equal standing as a State within the Union.

Horace Greeley had not yet been born, and it would be decades before he would write this famous phrase in his 1865 *New York Tribune* article: "Go West, young man, go West and grow up with the country." However, even in the late eighteenth century, there was government land to be explored and settled in the West. You could say that "the West" had a new definition during each decade of our country's history. As one scholar put it, "At different times it was on the banks of the Charles River, the Connecticut, and on the Hudson; on the shores of the Great Lakes, in the Mississippi valley, on the tops of the Rockies, and it stopped at the Pacific only because it could go no farther."

When the Northwest Territory opened its borders to American expansion, there was a corresponding movement to guarantee the spiritual welfare of this new area. At the time there were still relatively few churches in the nation. Massachusetts was probably above the norm, and in 1798 its tally showed eleven Episcopal churches, sixty-eight Baptist, three hundred thirty Congregational, three Universalist, six Quaker, and one Roman Catholic church. Religion, however, was an important part of normal life across the country. Godly people from many denominations began to organize in order to meet the anticipated spiritual needs of people in the new territory, and this new "Home Missionary" movement grew rapidly.

Nineteenth century religious historian Joseph B. Clark recorded the story of the American Home Missionary movement, and he described its beginnings during the opening of the Northwest Territory. "Contributions were taken up in all the churches, enabling ministers to go out on short tours, preaching and organizing churches...It cannot be too often and gratefully noted that the Congregationalists of New England, the Presbyterians and Reformed churches of the middle section, and the Baptists of Massachusetts started to do the same thing at about the same time." From that time onward, there was hardly any western section which was not touched by these itinerant missionary preachers. As Clark put it, "There is scarcely a western State which the home missionary army has not entered while it was yet a Territory and usually in the first and feeblest state of its settlement."

Frontier conditions in the Northwest Territory were just as rugged as in any unsettled wilderness that Americans pioneered, either before or since. There were unbelievable struggles and hardships to be endured by the men, women, and children who moved into the territory. But this was a land of opportunity, and many hardy souls took up the challenge. These families typically brought their religion with them, and those who came as pioneering pastors would face the same hardships as the members of their flock.

While the Northwest Territory was in the first stages of settlement, another event occurred which changed the face of the nation and added fuel to the home missionary fire. The French Revolution had brought Napoleon Bonaparte into power, and Napoleon turned his attention to his holdings in the New World. In October 1802 France revoked America's right to export its goods through the port of New Orleans, which meant the loss of nearly forty percent of the American

*Pioneer family standing near their sod house. They had each other, their mule, their land, and their faith.*

Courtesy of Library of Congress Prints and Photographs Division.

export trade. President Thomas Jefferson sent his ambassador to France to negotiate the purchase of New Orleans, authorizing as much as ten million dollars for the sale.

Meanwhile, however, several events turned against France, and Napoleon could no longer afford to station troops in North America to protect his interests. At that time Napoleon needed money more than he needed an unsettled wilderness halfway around the world. He ordered his foreign minister to sell not only New Orleans but all of the Louisiana Territory to the United States for approximately fifteen million dollars. The US Senate ratified the treaty in December 1803, and the Louisiana Territory came under the control of the United States government.

There was great excitement over the Louisiana Purchase, but no one knew exactly what the United States had acquired. Some of the boundary lines were very vague and the territory had not been well explored, so Jefferson convinced Congress to appropriate funds for the Lewis and Clark expedition in 1804. This expedition crossed the continental divide in the northern ranges and journeyed to the Pacific Ocean and back, searching in vain for a waterway to use as a northwest passage.

In 1806 Zebulon Pike was commissioned to cross the Great Plains to explore the south-central mountain regions, and by 1812 the Santa

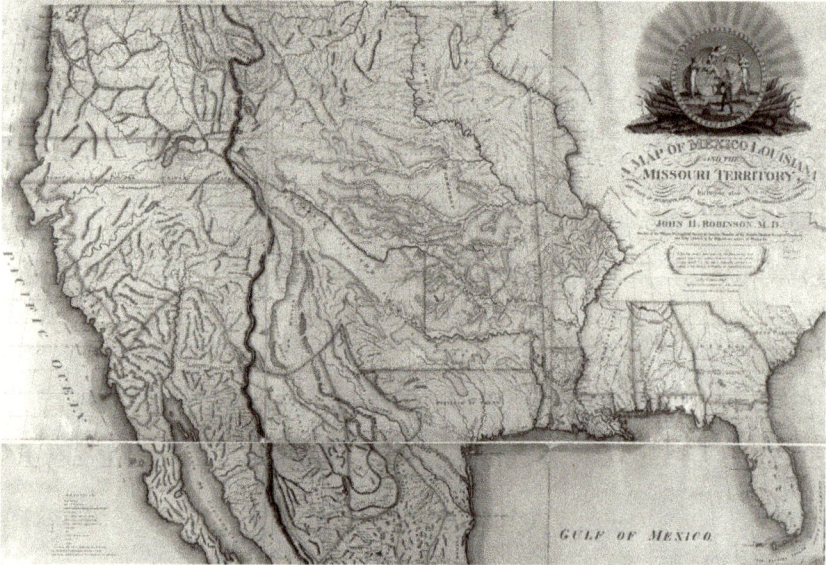

*1819 US government map of Mexico, Louisiana, and Missouri Territories.*
Courtesy of Library of Congress Prints and Photographs Division.

Fe Trail was first used as a commercial road between the United States and the northern capital of Spanish (later Mexican) territory. One historian put the Louisiana Purchase into perspective when he said, "The war of the Revolution gave us freedom; that of 1812 gave us commercial independence; but the purchase of Louisiana changed the national center of gravity."

After the War of 1812 a steady stream of settlers began to move west across the Appalachian Mountains from the Atlantic coast. The possibility of owning more land offered greater opportunities for prosperity. All of these pioneering families faced an uncertain future, but they came with the confidence that in this new land everyone could find success if they were willing to work for it. Between 1810 and 1820 the population of the Northwest Territory doubled, and in a short period of time four new States were added to the Union there.

Missionary preachers from several denominations began working throughout the area that would eventually become the States of Ohio, Indiana, Illinois, Michigan, Wisconsin, and Minnesota. The Methodist Episcopal Church developed a system by which their pastors would ride a consistent route or circuit, and these circuit riding preachers had great success in reaching a larger number of people on the frontier. The Methodist Church experienced such growth that some have called the early nineteenth century the Age of Methodism. Other denominations quickly adopted similar systems for organizing their efforts.

As early as 1814 pioneering preachers had reached Missouri. This was the year that Samuel J. Mills and Daniel Smith were sent out by the Protestant missionary societies of Connecticut and Massachusetts. They traveled on horseback across Pennsylvania and Ohio, southern Indiana and Illinois, and finally reached St. Louis on the banks of the Mississippi River. When they arrived they found a village of about two thousand souls, seventy-five percent of whom were Catholic due to the previous influence of France and Spain. Mills and Smith preached what may have been the first Protestant sermons on that side of the Mississippi. Two years later Salmon Giddings followed in their footsteps, and after eighteen months of intense labor he established the first Presbyterian church in St. Louis.

The American Bible Society was founded in 1816 with the stated purpose of making the Bible available to every person, so that all people could have the benefit of its life-changing message in a language they understand. The American Bible Society provided the first Bibles in hotels, and later they produced the first pocket Bibles for soldiers during the American Civil War.

By the late 1820s the circuit riding preacher became a familiar figure throughout the region. Periodically a group of these missionaries would organize special events called "camp meetings" where well-known speakers would minister to large groups of people who came to camp in an area for a few days. Not only were churches established as a result of these gatherings, but schools and other community services were often organized at the same time.

In the sequence of town development, the first buildings erected were usually homes and stores. As several families gathered in an area, schools were then established to meet the needs of the children. Itinerant preachers often used school buildings as public meeting places for church services. When enough church members were available, a separate church building might be constructed. Since money was scarce on the frontier, most churches were simple, plain structures with few frills. Wood or coal stoves heated the interior, while kerosene lamps provided lighting. An attached stable was essential, since church attendance was an all-day event and families would come from miles around on horseback or in horse-drawn wagons. If the congregation wanted to be extravagant, they might buy windows for their church.

A church building was the pride of any community. Missionary historian Joseph B. Clark noted, "Every church planted by home missions has been the nucleus of devotion to law, order, moral living, and patriotic virtue." Nothing else could better indicate the permanence and success of a town. Churches were signs of civilization and social order in a community, and town promoters realized that more families could be attracted to the area if a church were present. As one writer expressed it, "A church building with tower or steeple, and perhaps even a bell, openly advertised that a town was a fit place for women and children to live." Once a permanent church was established in a town, the itinerant preachers would move farther west into more sparsely populated areas in need of their services.

On the early frontier east of the Mississippi River, missionary pastors and circuit riding preachers were gaining the kind of training they would eventually require to serve the needs of the area west of the Mississippi. Westward expansion continued to occur rapidly, and in 1820 the government commissioned Stephen H. Long to explore the Great Plains and central Rockies. In 1824 fur trapper Jedediah Smith, who was also a man of faith, documented the discovery of South Pass in what is now southwestern Wyoming. This route became the primary mountain crossing for the famous emigrant road known as the Oregon Trail. In that same year the American Sunday School Union was started in order to promote the founding of Sunday schools and to publish books so children would have good reading material in their homes. In 1826 the American Home Missionary Society was established as an interdenominational effort to send Protestant ministers throughout the West.

By the mid-1830s a wagon road had been cleared through the Rocky Mountains as far as Ft. Hall in Idaho. Even in rugged conditions crossing the mountains and plains, wagon trains often held religious services during their layovers along the way. In 1834, John K. Townsend was traveling in a group with Reverend Jason Lee, the well-known missionary to the Oregon country. Townsend wrote,

> The next day being the Sabbath, our good missionary Mr. Jason Lee was requested to hold a meeting, with which he obligingly complied. A convenient shady spot was selected in the forest adjacent, and the greater part of our men, as well as the whole of Mr. McKay's company, including the Indians, attended. The usual forms of the Methodist service, to which Mr. L. is attached, were gone through and were followed by a brief but excellent and appropriate exhortation by that gentleman. The people were remarkably quiet and attentive, and the Indians sat upon the ground like statues. Although not one

*1840s sketch of a wagon train traversing the Rocky Mountains.*
Courtesy of Library of Congress Prints and Photographs Division.

of them could understand a word that was said, they nevertheless maintained the most strict and decorous silence, kneeling when the preacher kneeled and rising when he rose, evidently with a view of paying him and us a suitable respect.

A meeting for worship in the Rocky mountains is almost as unusual as the appearance of a herd of buffalo in the settlements. A sermon was perhaps never preached here before, but for myself I really enjoyed the whole scene. It possessed the charm of novelty, to say nothing of the salutary effect which I sincerely hope it may produce. Mr. Lee is a great favorite with the men, deservedly so, and there are probably few persons to whose preaching they would have listened with so much complaisance. I have often been amused and pleased by Mr. L.'s manner of reproving them for the coarseness and profanity of expression which is so universal amongst them. The reproof, although decided, clear and strong, is always characterized by the mildness and affectionate manner peculiar to the man. And although the good effect of the advice may not be discernible, yet it is always treated with respect and its utility acknowledged.

At a later time on the same trail another western traveler, Evans S. McComas of Iowa, described the religious services conducted during his wagon train excursion. "Had preaching in our corral by Capt. Bristle, the fighting Capt. of the Iowa City train. Had a sermon from the 8th chapt and 28th verse of Romans. It was a curious group for to be at church, the men with their Bowie knives and revolvers in their belts, dressed in shirtsleeves and buckskin pants." Informal services like these were common in groups traveling across the West.

Between 1842 and 1848, John C. Fremont led several government expeditions to explore and map more of the Far West between the Mississippi River and the Pacific coast. The 1846 Mexican War and the 1848 Treaty of Guadalupe Hidalgo brought all of this land into the United States, vastly expanding the territory that was open to settlement and to the home missionary movement. In January 1848, while constructing a diversion canal for Sutter's new sawmill in California, James Marshall discovered gold in the American River. News of this discovery touched off the California gold rush, and by 1849 almost 100,000 men flooded that region in search of riches.

The Kansas-Nebraska Act of 1854 opened vast new lands for permanent settlement on the Great Plains. Prior to this the region was little more than a "No Man's Land" to be traversed in order to reach the ultimate destinations of New Mexico or the Pacific coast. With the passage of this act, however, there was an almost immediate migration of families onto the Great Plains west of the Mississippi River. The home missionaries who pioneered the eastern frontier then moved into this new area and began using the same methods they had perfected earlier.

In 1858, one decade after the California rush, gold was also discovered in the mountains of the Pike's Peak region in what is now Colorado. As had happened in California, by the spring of 1859 thousands of men poured into the mountains in search of riches. Wherever discoveries were made, miners flooded the area and towns sprang up almost overnight. They often began as tent cities, but log cabins and board shacks quickly replaced tents as more permanent year-round structures. In areas where no official government existed, citizens sometimes organized "vigilance committees" to maintain peace and enforce justice against law-breakers. Life in the mining camps was rugged, but most of the residents were law-abiding and determined to make their towns into reputable communities.

Joseph B. Clark described the progress of the home missionaries:

> With the first considerable movement of population toward Colorado, the home missionary took the trail. Two years before Territorial organization, in 1859, open-air meetings were held at Gregory Diggings by Lewis Hamilton, and a union church composed of all denominations was formed. One year later, G.W. Fisher, a Methodist, organized a church at Central City, so called because it was the center of the gold mining region. A church of the same order was

*Leslie's Illustrated Newspaper article in the mid-1800s describing new mines discovered in the Rocky Mountains.*

Courtesy of Library of Congress Prints and Photographs Division.

also organized at Black Hawk in 1862. Presbyterian churches were gathered at Central City and Black Hawk in 1863. The American Home Missionary Society opened the first Congregational church of the Territory in Central City in 1863...Baptists began in 1864, closing in 1879. More than one Episcopal church at the same place had a similar fate. Such records are not unusual in mining regions where the people come and go, and often more frequently go than come.

William Crawford was pastor of the Congregational Church at Central City, Colorado, and in 1863 he remarked, "Perhaps there are some who think our society is so rude and wicked that there is no living here in comfort. Wicked enough and rude enough it is, but not wholly so. In few places will one meet with more well-informed and cultivated people or with pleasanter families. Our people demand and can appreciate good preaching; many of them have been accustomed to the best."

The American Civil War intervened, but afterward the nation continued moving westward. The transcontinental railroad was completed by 1869, and this sparked further development throughout the region. As each new area was opened for exploitation or settlement, a familiar pattern of events occurred. Tent cities would be followed by frame buildings and ultimately by structures of brick and stone. Schools and churches would be built. Periods of "boom" and "bust" were repeated in the economy, within political parties, and even in the weather patterns. Many of the small settlements established to take advantage of opportunities for mining, logging, ranching, and farming appeared and disappeared with these cycles.

Through it all, the itinerant pastors and pioneer preachers continued to work among their people. How did they get there? What hardships did they face? What kept them going? We can find the answers to these questions by allowing these remarkable people to tell their own stories in the pages that follow.

# Preachers Answer the Call

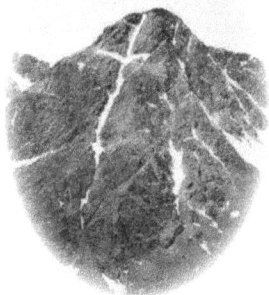

*"Bring me men to match my mountains, Bring me men to match my plains, Men with empires in their purpose, And new eras in their brains."*
—Sam Walter Foss,"The Coming American" (July 4, 1894)

*"How will they preach unless they are sent?"* (Romans 10:15)

As the call went out for "men to match my mountains" there were many, both young and old, who responded. Only time would tell whether each one was actually fit for the rugged life of a pioneer preacher. Some made the grade and stayed the course, while others returned almost immediately to the security of their eastern homes.

In the last chapter we were introduced to Jason Lee, a young Canadian minister who was chosen to lead a mission to the Flathead Indians in 1833. The circumstances surrounding this mission were remarkable because it was actually begun in response to a request by the Flathead themselves for someone to bring the "Book of Heaven" to their people. Their delegation traveled to St. Louis where they found their old friend General William Clark, then the Superintendent of Indian Affairs. In answer to this call, Jason Lee not only traveled to Oregon to establish a mission and school, but he also was instrumental in organizing the first territorial government in that region.

At about this time another young man, John Lewis Dyer, was growing to manhood in the Northwest Territory. Born on his family's home-

*Reverend Jason Lee, Missionary to Oregon*

*John Lewis Dyer,*
*Methodist Minister*

stead in Ohio in 1812, Dyer attended a Methodist camp meeting in 1832 at which he was converted. The following year he married a devout Methodist girl and their thirteen-year marriage produced five children before his wife died in 1847 after their move to the Wisconsin frontier. It seemed that the world had come to an end for Dyer. Not only was he a widower with young children to raise, but his money had run out, leaving him almost destitute. In order to raise funds Dyer worked as a lead miner in Wisconsin, which enabled him to pay some of his debts and purchase grave markers for his late wife and the infant daughter who shortly followed her. In 1850 he was granted a preaching license in the Methodist Episcopal Church and began to ride the frontier circuits in Wisconsin and Minnesota.

Meanwhile, the Mexican-American War had ended, and several home missionaries traveled to New Mexico. The first to arrive in the area was a Baptist minister in 1849, though he was essentially a military chaplain ministering on US Army posts and traveling with the troops as they moved from place to place. In 1850 the Missionary Society of the Methodist Episcopal Church sent its first missionary to New Mexico. Reverend E.G. Nicholson arrived in Santa Fe around the same time as another minister sent by the Presbyterians. Nicholson found conditions difficult and returned home shortly after his appointment. The Presbyterian minister moved to southwestern New Mexico and started a small ranch and store.

Almost as soon as the Kansas-Nebraska Act of 1854 had been passed, home missionaries began arriving in Kansas Territory. One of the first on the scene was Samuel Y. Lum who had been commissioned by the American Home Missionary Society to establish a Con-

*Congregational*
*Minister Samuel Y.*
*Lum of Kansas*

gregational church in the new city of Lawrence on the banks of the Kansas River. Lum traveled from his home in Middletown, New York, and was credited with preaching the first formal sermon in Kansas Territory. A month after his arrival he organized Plymouth Congregational Church which met in a mud brick boarding house, where people were called to meetings by ringing a large dinner bell.

Lum recorded his first impressions of this early Kansas frontier settlement on the bluff near the river:

> The town seemed smaller than I expected to find it. Every house and shanty, sod cabin and tent was filled to its utmost capacity. They were not the driftwood of the frontier, but people who had come with a purpose. Business and professional men had left their business, and come to this far country under the inspiration of an idea. College students just graduated, had turned their backs upon the career they had marked out for themselves, and come to Kansas at the call of freedom. It was no uncommon thing to find college graduates and men of culture driving a team of horses in the street, or chopping logs in the woods, or living in a shake shingle shanty far out on the prairie.

Just as Samuel Lum was sent to Kansas by the Congregationalists, the Methodists had sent William H. Goode to explore Kansas and Nebraska. At the time, Goode was in his mid-forties and had extensive experience as a circuit riding preacher and missionary to the Indians in the Northwest Territory states. He grew ill as he started this tour of the territories, and he continued to be sick and weak during his entire circuit. However, he faithfully discharged his duties, struggling to travel across the prairies and to preach wherever he could gather a crowd of settlers. Afterward he reported, "The number of actual residents in the territories I found to be smaller than generally supposed...There were not at that time five hundred families settled in the entire Territories of Kansas and Nebraska." But growth was expected, and Goode completed his report by recommending that two missionaries be sent to each territory. Little did he know that he himself would shortly be appointed to return to that very frontier.

In 1857 the entire nation experienced a financial panic that dramatically affected life on the frontier. Writing from Minnesota, John Dyer explained:

> The financial crash of 1857 was fully upon us. I had given forty acres of land toward the church, which was a large share of all I had. Unfortunately several of us went security for a man in order to help him bring a sawmill into the neighborhood, supposing him to be reliable. But he failed and as it turned out his father owned all the property, and the security had to be paid. I had no money, and so gave the mortgage on thirty-eight acres more to secure my note. When the mortgage was foreclosed, the father of the man deeded the land to

the debtor's wife! This, with some other misfortunes, and not receiving enough the two preceding years to support me and my family... suffice it to say I was financially bust. I actually sold my mule to pay a debt, and started on foot to my circuit, visiting all the houses and talking to the people on the importance of their salvation.

This nationwide financial crash was one of the reasons the 1858 discovery of gold in the Pike's Peak region became so important. Thousands of men were desperate for money, and the risk of braving the Great Plains and Rocky Mountains seemed a small price to pay for the chance to improve their current impoverished condition.

Even before there was an organized government in the Rocky Mountains, the eastern authorities of the Methodist Episcopal Church were planning for the spiritual welfare of the Pike's Peak region. William H. Goode described their concern: "The golden treasures beginning to be revealed in the region of the Rocky Mountains were inviting large numbers of our citizens and many of our Church members to these inhospitable and hitherto unfrequented parts." The church was faithful to its pioneer calling and wanted to send missionaries immediately, but there were no available volunteers. The presiding bishop even made a personal appeal to Goode, but Goode declined to go and no one was sent. Within a few weeks, however, Goode changed his mind. He had once commented that "men who have spent a few years upon the frontier are rarely afterward satisfied elsewhere. So it has proved with me." Here he described his change of heart:

*Methodist Minister William H. Goode*

> Other providential changes followed in rapid succession, which, painful as they were in themselves, nevertheless opened the way to an acceptance of the proposed work. The stream of emigration was rolling by me daily, and the desire revived to go and spend a season on the Plains, in the mountain solitudes, and the camps of the miners...The appointment was made, and the next morning the whip was cracked for a trip to the Pike's Peak and Cherry Creek Mission... In the midst of these scenes I passed my fifty-second birthday.

As his associate in the work, Goode was given the young probationary preacher at Rock Bluff mission—twenty-four year old Jacob Adriance. Having little formal education and no preaching experience,

Adriance had left his home in New York to go west in 1857. He had arrived in Omaha and was assigned to a circuit of eight stops along the Missouri River where he rode on horseback as many as 300 miles each month to preach at the settlements. He proved himself eager to serve, powerful in prayer, and an especially good song leader.

What follows is Goode's account of the feverish migration to the gold fields:

> The stampede was taking place. Multitudes in the States, allured by the reports, had resolved to visit the place where gold could be gathered from the brooks and the sands without measure, enriching themselves at once. The golden vision flitted before their eyes and obscured all else. Money was borrowed, lands were sold or mortgaged, other property sacrificed, wife and children placed upon a scanty allowance to live upon the hope of future abundance, and fathers, brothers, and sons were en route for Pike's Peak. Banners floated, revolvers were flourished, the pick and pan were ostentatiously displayed as emblems of future and certain acquisition, and light and merry hearts sang or whistled along the westward roads... Some were thoughtful, considerate, prudent men, but the great mass were inconsiderate, rash, and reckless, with poor teams, crazy wagons, and almost without harness. A large number of men actually harnessed themselves to hand carts to draw their tools, provisions, and equipage, almost a thousand miles over an uninhabited plain. Some undertook the journey with wheelbarrows, while not a few hazarded the entire trip on foot, lugging their scanty supplies on their shoulders...Some went nearly through, others half way, but by far the larger number only a short distance into the Territory, encountering severe rains, snow storms, and other hardships. Enough, however, reached Cherry Creek to produce a heavy pressure upon the few inhabitants there. Provisions were scarce. No employment for hire. The Cherry Creek diggings were yielding unsatisfactory returns...Pike's Peak banners were exchanged for pictures of "the elephant" and other emblems and mottoes of defeat. Such was the state of things as the stampede was then passing by me.

Even before Goode and Adriance arrived in the mountains, a carpenter and wagon maker named George W. Fisher began holding services in Denver City. Fisher had been a Methodist "lay" leader, and the city's founder, General William Larimer, a devout Presbyterian, asked him to conduct a meeting the first Sunday they arrived in the Pike's

Peak region. Larimer's eighteen-year-old son described the services in his diary:

> November 21, 1858: A morning service. The congregation was small although Mr. Fisher and my father went around and invited everyone to attend. No church bells to ring, no finely draped ladies, no choir. No pews to sit in, but seated on buffalo robes spread on the ground, with both the Jones and Smith squaws the only women present. Fisher, father, myself, and perhaps six or eight others held the first religious service ever held in the country. In the opposite end of the cabin I could hear the money jingle where the gambling was going on at the same time that Mr. Fisher was preaching.

When Goode and Adriance arrived in early July 1859, the settlement contained thirty-one saloons but no churches, schools, hospitals, libraries, or banks. The Pollack House Hotel was one of the few structures built of sawn lumber, so on their first Sunday they spoke to a few area residents who had assembled there. Goode preached in the morning, while Adriance spoke in the afternoon. They initially found it difficult to gather an audience, until they adopted the practice described here by Goode:

> As the hour approached, finding our congregation likely to be rather slim, I went around to the crowds, however engaged, personally invited them in, and at length succeeded in obtaining a tolerable assemblage...Whenever necessary I have posted written notices, then mounted a mule and rode around the evening previous to ranches, houses, booths, tents, wagons, liquor stands, and card tables, and from all these places have invited them out. But one of the most effective means, after all, was to sing them up, and in this I have a most efficient aid in the fine musical powers of brother Adriance. There is power in song, and perhaps nowhere else more felt and seen than here among those so long absent from religious associations. We never fail to collect a group in a short time.

During his brief stay in Denver City, Goode also preached in a large cloth pavilion called "the round tent," a well-known gambling location. The inhabitants graciously ceased their activity long enough for the service, and Goode reported, "I treated them kindly, and they in turn listened respectfully and allowed me without offense to preach home truths to them in all plainness and fidelity. They treated me courteously and agreed to let me preach there again." Afterward Goode and

Adriance pulled up stakes and set their course for the mountain mining camps. Here Goode describes their journey:

> We—brother Adriance and myself—set off for the mountain diggings, he upon his saddle horse and I upon the back of my faithful mule, Bob, a noble steed over fifteen hands high, safe and sure, but like others of his species, somewhat self-willed...Leaving the gulch, we crossed several high spurs difficult to ascend and descend. Soon after we entered a small, narrow valley affording for a time an easier ascent and freer breathing. Here the scenery became magnificent. Masses of rock on either hand rise to an almost bewildering height, crowned with lofty evergreens...We sought a secluded vale, picketed our animals, built our fire, took our frugal meal, and laid ourselves down to rest. The night passed well but for the extreme cold, for which our packed bedroll was insufficient. It is no boast of superior industry to say that coffee was taken early and we were again packed and in the saddle.

They arrived safely at Gregory Diggings and immediately made the acquaintance of several Methodist church members who had come to work the mines. They also met many Presbyterians, Baptists, and Congregationalists who were glad to have preachers in the camp. Sunday morning services were held on a crowded dusty street with a large group of attentive participants. In the afternoon they retired to a high mountain ridge for an informal "experience meeting" where Goode reported that "the vows

*Methodist Minister Jacob Adriance*

of reconsecration, the weepings, the rejoicings, will not be forgotten in time." They had gathered almost one hundred people for their church by that time, and they officially organized the "Rocky Mountain Mission" by recording the names of all those applying for membership. George W. Fisher was left in charge of that group, while Goode and Adriance moved on to other camps.

> We took the beaten trail down a gulch, over almost impracticable spurs and crags, so steep that when we stopped to corral at noon we could scarcely find a spot where our baggage would lie without rolling to the bottom. The practice is to take the wagon or cart as far as possible, then unload and pack through on the backs of beasts or the shoulders of men, to the otherwise inaccessible places, leaving the

wagon cabled to a pine tree using a log chain, lest it should incontinently rush to the bottom by the power of gravitation.

Goode and Adriance encountered fierce thunderstorms, raging creeks, treacherous trails, and mile after mile of new diggings. "On every gulch, ravine, and creek are seen tents, mines, sluices, and the mountainsides literally pocketed with holes in the search for quartz veins." Most of the inhabitants looked as rough and rugged as their buildings and equipment. However, every once in a while they encountered a site which looked orderly and appealing. Goode described the apparent reason:

> Now and then a tent or shack is passed where superior order and neatness reign. Soon all is explained. A neatly-attired lady appears as the presiding genius of the institution, moving gracefully about her domestic avocations. Left by themselves, men degenerate rapidly, become rough, harsh, slovenly. Men need the restraining, elevating influence of female society. Women bear up under the hardships of frontier life as well or better than men. There are more females here than I should have supposed, especially in the towns.

Even though many of the men had rough exteriors, the inward character of the vast majority of them tended toward positive morality. This was well-expressed by Goode:

> A tribute is especially due the morals of the Rocky Mountain miners in one particular. "Our Creek runs Clear on the Sabbath," said one to me, alluding to Clear Creek which washes the product of the mines. Turbid and dark, unfit for use during the six working days, on the Sabbath its pure and invigorating current, fresh from the mountain snows, flows bright and silvery. The thousands of laborers above have suspended their toil and are enjoying a season of rest on God's holy day...Thousands more are coming. Many of them are our brethren, Christians; some are humble seekers of religion; some are struggling to break away from habits of dissipation and rise to a better life.

Adriance and Goode made their return journey through the mountains, "along a narrow defile, overhanging precipices above, deep gulch of the stream beneath, and we leave the diggings." Descending rapidly, they finally reached their original camp in the Platte River valley, "*minus* some mule flesh and some articles of personal equipage, *plus* some lessons in mountain traveling."

Almost immediately upon their return to Denver City, Goode began serving as chaplain for the State of Jefferson Constitutional Convention, an abortive attempt to attain statehood for what eventually became Colorado almost two decades later. Goode wrote that "the effort for a State I think premature, and there are in my judgment insuperable barriers to its present success, independent of the smallness of their population." His assessment was accurate, but during this time he and Jacob Adriance productively formed the basis for a vital ministry in the area. They purchased town lots as sites for possible church buildings, and they continued to preach and organize meetings of members. As a result of their six week exploration of the territory, they had established churches in Golden, Central City, and Denver.

At this point, William Goode returned to his assignment in Nebraska, leaving Adriance in charge of all their work in the Rocky Mountains. It is little wonder that young Jacob Adriance recorded the following entry in his diary: "They left me and a part of my things under a tree at camp. Brother Reitze came down with a wagon and got them about three o'clock. I reached town about five. Moved into a cabin. Got my things mostly together. Had supper all alone, bread and stewed peaches. I feel a little lonesome." Adriance described his cabin as a somewhat bare and primitive structure:

> The logs were hewn, corners trimmed, no chimney, fronted west, a double-sash window in the east which had been imported from New Mexico. The roof was clapboarded with split shingles, not unlike barrel staves, then covered with dirt, through which the stove pipe extended from the little iron stove in the southeast corner. Rough boards for a door, dirt floor. I covered the ground with hay, made a table, bedstead, two stools, and with a little camp stove, a tin plate, cup, knife and fork, two blankets, and a buffalo robe, I commenced housekeeping.

Despite the loneliness and isolation, Adriance got busy with his ministry work. He held prayer meetings in his cabin, established a new church in Boulder City, conducted regular Sunday services everywhere along his circuit, and held class meetings after preaching wherever he found a few dedicated people present. Adriance once met a man who did not have anything to eat, and he brought him to his cabin to provide food and shelter—keeping him for a month.

In Goode's absence, Adriance was elected Chaplain of the House for the provisional government legislature of the new Territory. This was quite an honor for the twenty-four year old circuit riding preacher. When George Fisher came down from the mountains to spend the winter on the plains, he and Adriance organized the first cooperative, non-denominational Union Sunday School for people of all faiths. Both children and adults attended these meetings, which Adriance held in his log cabin every year during his ministry in the Rockies. In subsequent years he traveled his circuit on foot because it became too expensive to keep a pony.

In 1859 William Goode published this astute assessment of the future of the Rocky Mountain region:

> From the success of a few miners, it will not do to infer positively the future fate of the vast multitudes who may hereafter be allured from their homes to engage in the doubtful enterprise. Doubtful and precarious it always is. The history of the mining enterprise, so far as I have studied it, has been anything but gratifying in its results to the great mass of those personally engaged in it...What further and richer fields yet remain unrevealed, or when the enterprise may be checked by unexpected failures, I cannot divine. But the problems will be solved. The exploration will be made of probably hundreds of miles of the mountain range, occupying years to come. These mountain ranges will teem with hardy enterprising inhabitants, a State government, and perhaps several, will be found midway between the Mississippi and the Pacific. Railway facilities will be demanded with an urgency that will compel their construction, and the great break between the now disjointed portions of our continent will be filled up, not with an agricultural people, for the country will not permit this, but with capitalists who will...enhance the value of the lands and thus contribute to the general prosperity.

A quick fast-forward through history proves that these words were almost prophetic. The exploration and development of the Rocky Mountain region continued almost exactly as Goode predicted, and the spiritual welfare of the expanding population continued to draw men to match these mountains.

# How Dyer Came to the Mountains

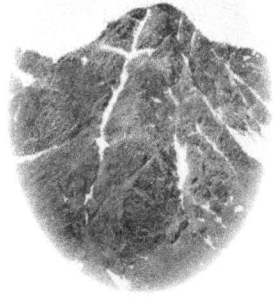

In the last chapter we were introduced to John Lewis Dyer, a Methodist preacher from the Northwest Territory region. At the age of thirty-eight he had been granted a provisional preaching license and assigned a circuit to ride. However it was not until Dyer reached his mid-forties that he passed his examination and was granted full status as a missionary preacher.

Probationary candidates followed a course of studies in what was called "Brush College." This meant that, whether the preacher was riding horseback or lodging in a woodland cabin, he would try to find a few hours for study whenever and wherever he could. The examination was administered by a group of experienced leaders from the denominational board, and the probationers always approached this testing with fear and trembling. The new candidates called this process "going through the flint mill."

John Dyer finally passed his examinations and was ordained on September 2, 1855, in the Wisconsin Conference. This fully qualified him to officiate baptisms, communions, marriages, and the burial of the dead. It was a significant and special milestone for John Lewis Dyer.

One of the challenges for the circuit riders was the strict commitment never to miss a preaching appointment. This meant traveling from place

*John L. Dyer,*
*Methodist Minister*

to place on foot or horseback, battling inclement weather and primitive trail conditions, and even confronting wild animals along the way. Here one of Dyer's contemporaries describes his encounter with a bear on his way to a preaching appointment:

> I traveled on foot. There were three reasons for this: first, I had no horse; secondly, I could not get to all of the work with a horse; thirdly, it would have been very hard to get feed for a horse. So for a year and a half I went to all my appointments on foot. One Sabbath I was traveling a piece of solid bush for two miles of the distance. When I got part way through I passed a little boy. A little further on a big black bear walked out into the road and took his stand right in front of me, and only a rod from where I stood. He faced me to all appearance with as little concern as a dog or pig would have done. The boy came up, and with a scream put his arms around me and cried out, "O, save me from the bear." I had not so much as a pocket knife with me. I saw at once the situation of things. I believed that I could get out of the way, but the boy could not do so. My resolve was taken in less time than it takes me to write it.
>
> I had read in books, and I had heard hunters say, that no animal can stand the human eye. I resolved to test this theory. I had no trouble to catch his eye, and I looked sternly into it, with all the determination and will that I was capable of showing. For a while, perhaps five minutes, it was not possible to say which seemed least concerned, the bear or myself. But after some time I saw that his eye began to quiver. I said to myself, "I have got him." In a few minutes he turned and walked out of sight. Twenty years after this I was stopping overnight in the neighborhood. The church stood less than six rods from the spot where I had met the bear in the woods twenty years ago. I mentioned the circumstances in a few remarks that I was called upon to make. After the meeting closed a man came up to me and said, "I have often heard that boy tell about the bear and the man that looked it out of countenance, but we never knew who it was.

There were many times when John Dyer relied on his determination and ingenuity to make it to a preaching appointment. On one occasion it had rained throughout the night, and when he started his journey in the morning he found the nearby stream was out of its banks and water covered all the low ground. Here he recounts his perilous crossing and the subsequent preaching appointment:

I concluded to try to cross, and went upstream to take advantage of the current. I started in water knee-deep; all at once the horse and rider were under, except my head and neck. I supposed my horse would rise and swim, but either he did not know how or would not, for his head would not come up. Fortunately we reached where he could stand, the water over his back, but his head out. After crossing and once out of sight, I wrung out my clothes. I had an appointment about two miles distant. The man said he would have had a dozen to hear me, but the flood prevented it, so he had seven. I was all wet and had taken my boots off, and was drying my socks. The time came, and the poor Irishman said: "Can't we have a little preaching?" I said: "I can't put my boots on; would it do barefooted?" He said, "Just as well." I gave out a hymn and kneeled in prayer, and did the best I could barefooted.

Sometimes the inclement weather was the least of their worries on the frontier. Most settlers lived in isolation, and there were very few amenities for their assistance. During one very difficult winter, an entire region experienced a series of devastating disease outbreaks. Dyer tells the story of this tragic period:

It seemed that we had more than our share of difficulties to settle, and in addition in the winter the smallpox broke out at Centerville in one of our best societies, and two members died. We could have no services for months. Then the cholera broke out in different places on the work, and cut off nearly twenty. This cast a gloom and fear over almost all classes of people. At Wiota all of one family died, and the neighbors got together and burnt the house with the dead bodies in it...In cases of burial, it seemed that the people thought the bodies could not be interred soon enough after death, and it was doubtful if some were not buried alive.

At Fayette, where we lived, three of one family died; only one little girl was left. Brother and Sister Benson, both members of our church, were called away. The mother was taken first. I visited her. She was in extreme pain, but was resigned to the will of God. In twenty-four hours she died. I was with her to the last. It was warm weather, and at nine o'clock in the evening we sent out for help, as she was a large woman. Only Aunt Polly Journey came. My sister was at home with my sick daughter, and I sent for her. Nathan Woodberry also came, and as the bedroom was too small, we carried the corpse out in front of the house and laid her out. Two or three had been dispatched to dig the grave. Her husband had sent to have a coffin, as he feared the people would want to bury her without one. Mr. Woodberry got a wagon and team and we went a half mile for the coffin, which was not quite done. This was Monday night, and I had preached three times the day before, so I lay down in the shavings and slept till the coffin was done. About day-break there were just enough of us to perform the burial of the poor woman suddenly called to death. Just before she breathed her last, their little boy was taken down, and within twenty-four hours he was buried.

On the next Monday I was sent for, to go and see Brother Benson. He was at his brother-in-law's, one and a half miles away, and had the cholera. I carried him some medicine, as the doctor would not go. We worked over him all day till about dark. His brother-in-law and I were the only ones to attend on him. We tried to encourage him, but he seemed to expect to die. He suffered intensely, and about dark breathed his last. His brother-in-law said: "You are older than I; you must stay and I will go for help." He went to the village, and no one would go. Sister Nancy Smith, a good and brave woman, said if the men would not go, she would raise some women to go. This stirred two men to go with Woodberry.

By the time they got the coffin it was dark. It was a rainy night, with thunder rumbling. I was left to myself and laid him out as best I could, wrapping him in a sheet, and sat down on the opposite side of the room, musing all alone. Just then he began to move his hands and one foot. I went to him and spoke to him, but he was dead; the cramp worked on his nerves. He moved one hand up to his shoulder, and the other downward; raised one knee six inches. His limbs could not be moved any more. All the light we had was a little old tin lamp—hog's lard for oil—and that almost gone. As it was after midnight, I looked toward the road. It was raining, but presently I saw a light coming, and they drove up to the door.

They came in and asked me what we had better do. There were men digging the grave, but I told them I did not wish to bury him so soon nor at night. We put the corpse into the coffin, and laid the cover over all but his face; then we went home and slept. In the morning I took my horse and buggy, and asked several to go with me, but without success. At last we met Brother Horace Woodworth, a Free-will Baptist preacher, and he did not refuse. He and Brother John Ethridge and Brother John Roberts took the corpse in their wagon, and buried it in daytime beside his wife and child, assured that they were safely landed together in the heavenly home. I would say just here that I had always been afraid of the cholera till it came where I was, but then I could discharge any duty that I was called to perform without any fear whatever...I felt, and still feel, great thankfulness to God for his sustaining grace.

Through the years of his frontier ministry, Dyer had escaped from numerous dangerous situations and had been spared from serious illness. But during his most remote assignment in western Minnesota he began to experience eye problems. Both of his eyes became infected and the condition gradually worsened until he could hardly see. In the evenings he would stand near a coal oil lamp and apply a strong caustic paste to his eyes by turning his eyelids over. In the morning he needed to soak his crusted eyelids with water before he could partially open them. The expected outcome was total blindness, and Dyer could not imagine a future for a blind itinerant preacher who could no longer travel, read, or study the Bible.

In the spring of 1861, at the age of almost fifty, Dyer decided to leave his ministry and make a visit to his children. Times were still hard financially, and when he arrived at his daughter's home he attempted to pay off his outstanding debts. He had put up security on two loans, so he paid one and gave his house and some town lots for over four hundred dollars on another. This left him with a horse, saddle and bridle, a few books in a carpet bag, a change of linen, and fourteen dollars and seventy-five cents in coins. He still owed about seven hundred dollars, and his creditors wanted to take his horse as partial payment. Dyer was very low emotionally, and he lamented that "no man can realize just how I felt unless he has been in the same situation."

Elias Dyer, John's second son, had traveled west with the stampede to the Rocky Mountains, and he was then a clerk in a Denver store. John Dyer was determined to see him one last time, so he made it his goal to journey by faith toward the mountains.

I had made up my mind to see Pike's Peak, that was, if I could see at all, as I had to wet my eyes and wipe them to get them open every morning. My friends advised me not to go. Added to blindness, my means were scanty, but I had made up my mind to go—if I did not starve on the way—and felt that my Heavenly Father would provide, and that my bread and water were sure.

As I left Minnesota I could but reflect on the six years passed in that new country. First, I counted up over five hundred converts whom I had seen at the altar. I had been the first preacher in many places, and in this I praised God for his goodness in making me his instrument in doing some good. Looking at my financial condition, I could see no way out, but I had given all my property up, and had one consolation, and that was that I intended to wrong no one, and cared less for what was gone than that I was unable to pay at once all claims against me. I held myself fully committed to pay every cent as soon as I could make it.

I rode that day forty-seven miles and stopped for the night. From that to Newton, Iowa, I made fifty miles a day, and rested Sunday at that place. While at breakfast, the landlord put my horse in a stall near a peck of corn, and she foundered almost to death. I led her a few miles and sold her for a gun, an old watch, and fifteen dollars, which was very little more than the saddle and bridle were worth. I stopped at Omaha, and there was a train of eighteen wagons starting for Pike's Peak. One of the men agreed to board me across for fifteen dollars, and haul my carpet sack and gun. I was to walk.

Dyer did indeed walk the six hundred miles across the Great Plains to see his son and the Rocky Mountains. Along the way, as opportunities presented themselves, he also continued to fulfill his calling to preach the "good news." The wagon train arrived in one settlement about ten o'clock on a Sunday morning, and Dyer was told they were holding a service. He stayed to listen, and they invited him to preach at the afternoon meeting. Figuring that it would be fairly easy to overtake a slow ox team, Dyer stayed through the day and then walked alone through the night to catch his wagon train.

Dyer would find that the further west he walked, the less his eyes seemed to bother him. By the time the mountains were glimpsed on the horizon, Dyer could almost make them out for himself. It seems that the clear, dry air on the prairie was beginning to heal and restore his vision. On June 20, 1861, the wagon train was approaching the foot of the mountains. Here Dyer describes the end of his journey across the Great American Desert:

Now we came to the last night on the plains. I had two pairs of pants, about half worn. I had left my pocket knife and purse in the pocket in the pair that was in the wagon that night, and when I took them out found the contents all gone. Well, the loss was small, as it was less than two dollars and a half, but it was all I had. I was consoled in the fact that I was no worse off than I would have been if it had been five thousand dollars. We stopped two miles up Cherry Creek above Denver. I took what I had in my carpet sack and, with my gun on my shoulder, walked into the town and met my son Elias who had come a year before.

Dyer thoroughly enjoyed the reunion with his son, Elias, who held a special place in his heart. They spent two weeks together, and visited with many other acquaintances whom they had known from the East. Dyer was asked to preach at Sunday services in Denver, but he was still eager to visit the Rocky Mountains themselves. A new excitement was stirring in a mining camp called Buckskin Joe at the foot of the Continental Divide, and Dyer immediately made plans for a visit. His time was short, since he was expecting to return eastward in the autumn if he could manage it.

I swapped my watch for about twenty dollars' worth of provisions—flour, bacon, sugar, coffee, and a few cans of fruit. My son gave me a buffalo skin and quilt for bedding. My mind was bent on a mountain trip, and no time to spare, as I thought of getting back by the last of September. The Phillips Lode at Buckskin Joe was the point of the greatest excitement at that time. I joined myself to a company which had a team. They hauled my stuff, and I started on foot for another hundred miles...We began to ascend the mountains on the 4th of July, 1861, and as it was my first mountain trip, I was wonderfully interested. It was so different from what I supposed—timber, grass, shrubs of many kinds, strawberry vines in full bloom, with an occasional view back across the plains.

*The town of Buckskin Joe, Colorado Territory, as it appeared in 1864.*
Courtesy of Denver Public Library Western History Collection: X-11927

We reached the head of the North Platte on Kenosha Hill. For over twenty miles up the canyon we had been shut out from seeing much of the world by the towering mountains on either side. We were well prepared, as we reached the top, to be astonished at the sight of South Park, which from this point is a view of grandeur never to be forgotten. Prairies, surrounded with high mountains and interspersed with pine groves and small peaks—a very Eden Park—are a sight seldom surpassed even in the Rocky Mountains. On the ninth day of July, we reached Buckskin Joe Camp, just two months from the day I left Lenora, Minnesota. My eyes had improved a little. Otherwise, I enjoyed good health after a tramp of over seven hundred miles on foot.

Almost as soon as he arrived in Buckskin Joe, Dyer realized that the buzzing mass of humanity in the gold camps was more in need of the "true riches of the gospel" than of any earthly golden treasure. He had not been officially commissioned to preach there, but he could not help himself—it was in his nature. He arrived on a Tuesday and the following Sunday he found a shady spot, pulled up a few logs for seating, and began preaching. That day he formed a Methodist class of twenty members, which was the first such group to be organized that high up in the mountains. Such pioneering efforts were to be the hallmark of Dyer's ministry in the years to come.

The mountain valley called South Park was like a hub from which spokes of mining activity radiated in all directions, and it was to become Dyer's ministry headquarters. He had assumed that his visit to the mountain camp of Buckskin Joe would be the final stop on his westward journey, but little did he realize that it was only the beginning of what God had planned for him. Instead of nearing the end of his journey and possibly the end of his life, Dyer was to have an additional forty years of mountain ministry in Colorado and New Mexico.

# The Snowshoe Itinerant

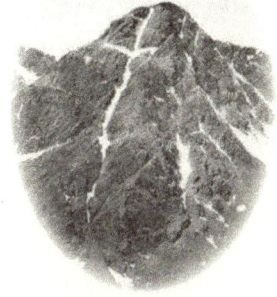

J ohn Dyer's plans to return east in September began to dim. There were several other mining camps near Buckskin Joe, and Dyer set out in August 1861 to visit them.

The first Sunday in August I walked eight miles to Montgomery to preach, and instead of finding a good number, all were out staking off claims but one man. He asked me to take dinner. We sat down on the ground to eat, as there was not a house, table, or stool in the place. From there I made my way up to Quartz Hill, just at timber line, where I preached to about thirty attentive hearers and felt that the Lord was with us. Walked back sixteen miles and held two services. The next Sabbath, visited Fairplay and preached to thirty who all gave good attention to the words spoken, as it was the first preaching there. On the 25th of August I tried to preach the first sermon in Mosquito by a camp fire, as there was no house at the time in the place. For nine weeks my house was made of poles and pine boughs, so thatched that they turned the rain after being well soaked one night.

Early in September Dyer learned that a boom town across the mountains to the west had been left without a preacher. The area was called California Gulch and the town was known as Oro City, named after the Spanish word for gold. This would be the place where Leadville would eventually spring up during a future silver mining boom. In order to get to Oro City, Dyer had to traverse a rugged mountain range over 13,000 feet in elevation. At these altitudes there really was no discernible trail, since the ground was covered with massive boulder fields, and freezing winds or snow squalls could occur year round. Dyer had heard of the difficulty in crossing, but he knew of the spiritual needs and decided to go.

On the 16th of September I set out for California Gulch, having been solicited previously to take charge of that mission by the pastor who supplied it. He agreed to have the presiding elder make the change, but he left in disgrace. I was left on my own resources, in a wilderness country, with six or seven members, and they were scattered over one hundred miles. My outfit was a buffalo skin and quilt, some crackers, a piece of bacon, a tin cup, and an oyster can—in all, thirty-seven and one half pounds to pack on my back. I now made my way up the range, about eight miles, to the top of the Mosquito Pass, the highest and hardest range I had then crossed. From here I could see the head of the Platte River, Arkansas, Blue River, and the head of the Grand River. Like the Garden of Eden, it was at least the starting point of all these mighty rivers. As I took a view of those gigantic mountain peaks and deep gorges, the thought came to me, if heaven is above then I am nearer to it than ever before. After prayer for our country on both sides, and for myself, alone on the dividing range of our great continent, I partook of my frugal stores and that night preached in California Gulch, now Leadville.

The excitement in Oro City was waning, and some of the prospectors were saying that "there was no longer much *oro* left in Oro." Many had left the area and moved farther west across the Continental Divide to the area around the Gunnison River valley. Dyer decided to visit those distant camps too, since all of the miners could use some good gospel preaching. This was the season for the golden aspen trees to paint the high valleys with color.

The next day I started alone for the Gunnison country, following an Indian trail. Had to wade the Arkansas. Took off my boots, and I thought the top of the cold water would cut my legs off. That day I saw for the first time the beautiful Twin Lakes. Had not heard of them before. My surprise may be imagined. My path was up Lake Creek, a perfect mountain wilderness, snowy ranges towering on either side. I had not seen a human being for several miles. Night was coming on, and I began to look for a camping place. I heard, just as the sun was sinking behind the snow-capped mountains, the sound of a bell and soon found five men. They had one burro to pack their food and blankets. I asked for lodging. They said: "If you can furnish your own accommodations, you can stay." I accepted. I had a paper with me with a sermon preached by Dr. Elliott in St. Louis. By the fire made of pine roots it was read, and you better believe it was a grand treat.

I reached Kent's Gulch where there were about one hundred men, one of whom had a family. He had raised his house, and was just covering it with poles, grass, and dirt. I told him I was a Methodist preacher and would like to preach in his house. He said: "You can, sir, when I get the roof on." It was announced for the next night, and nearly every man in the diggings came. There was a table and two benches. When the benches were full, the hearers sat on the ground all around the walls, and the next row against their knees, until every foot of space was filled. A more attentive crowd is seldom seen, and God's presence was manifest. This was the first effort in the way of preaching ever made in all the Gunnison country. One man arose and took a collection of about twenty dollars in gold dust, and gave me an invitation to come and preach again.

Dyer realized that the miners did not care for polished speeches from trained orators, but wanted their sermons delivered in plain words with sincere emotion. That kind of preaching gained a hearing, and that kind of preacher earned their respect. Fifty-year-old John Dyer was a perfect match for these men in the mountains. He often carried his own gold pan and shovel, he was not afraid of hard work, and he pitched in to lend a helping hand wherever he could. The mining camps and the prospectors were continually moving from place to place in search of paying minerals, and what they needed was an itinerant preacher like John Dyer who could keep up with them.

Sabbath, the 24th of September, I entered the town of Minersville and shall not forget the scene. One man was cutting and selling beef, others rolling logs down the hill, others covering their cabins, another building a chimney, and still others selling provisions and whiskey in a tent. From this standpoint I resolved to announce my appointment. The first man I spoke to was dressing some grouse. After salutation I said: "Did not you expect a Methodist preacher would be on hand as soon as you had chicken to eat?" "Well," he said, "I have heard that they were fond of chickens," and he gave me a welcome to take dinner with him. I stepped out to about the center of the camp and said: "O yes! O yes! O yes! There will be preaching at half past ten o'clock wherever the most people can be found together." One asked me who was going to preach. I made a bow and said: "I am going to try, with the help of God." He seemed much astonished, meeting such a hard-looking man. I invited him to come and hear preaching. The time arrived, and now came the tug of war, for the most people were around the grocery. Forty men and jacks, mules, and ponies. Just now the preacher began to sweat. It was hard to speak in such a place, not knowing that there was one in sympathy with him, but it must be done. I got in front of the tent, under the shade of a pine tree, and read the hymn, beginning to sing "Alas! And Did My Savior Bleed." As I tried in the old way to sing it, a number joined in and helped, but some were selling, others buying, and some packing their beasts. At the proper time I said: "Let us pray." After this the poor preacher began to feel better, and the people kept coming in until there were over one hundred. I was at the last camp east of California, and had the evidence that God was in the wilderness as well as in the city...A man came to me at the close, and invited me to take breakfast with him. He said it was the first sermon he had heard preached for eight years. They gave me about ten dollars.

Dyer had created his own unique "circuit" for preaching, and he traveled this route through the end of that year ministering to all of the miners in the camps. He still maintained a cabin at Buckskin Joe as his headquarters, but it had been weeks since he returned to it. Finally in January 1862 he determined to make the trip back over the 13,000-foot Mosquito Range.

I started alone for Buckskin Joe by the Weston Pass. At timber height I was met be a severe snow storm. I had a box of matches, but not one would burn. The prospect was frightful. I prayed and dedicated myself to God, and thought that by his grace I would try to pull through. For five or six hours I waded the waist-deep snow until, almost exhausted, I leaned up against a tree to rest. I never saw death and eternity so near as then. My life seemed to be at an end, but I resolved to keep moving, and when I could go no more, would hang up my carpet sack and write on a smooth pine tree my own epitaph—"Look for me in heaven." But through the goodness of God I reached the toll-gate about one hour after dark, and I shall never forget the kindness of the Swede who took me in and cared for me.

Many of the mountain residents had left their diggings to spend the winter in relative warmth at Denver, so in February 1862 Dyer decided to travel there to see his son and catch up on news from the East. There was a regular stagecoach from Buckskin Joe to Denver, but the fare was ten dollars and Dyer figured he could save money by walking the 100 miles. In a little over two days he arrived in Denver on a Saturday evening, and on Sunday he attended church wearing his only outfit—dirty and worn miner's clothes. Dressed as he was, he thought he would sit quietly in the back of the church and listen, but the leader of the service noticed him and shouted, "Come preach for me." Everyone turned toward Dyer and, since he could no longer hide, he agreed to speak. Later he commented, "I can say nothing about the sermon, only that I forgot all about poor clothes" as he faithfully preached his message. The next day the newspaper reported, "A reverend gentleman from California Gulch preached fervently and acceptably in the Methodist Church."

While in Denver, Dyer learned that his oldest son, Joshua, had enlisted in the Union Army and was fighting with Company H of the First Minnesota Volunteers. Jacob Adriance recruited Dyer for a trip to the mining camps near Central City where they held a quarterly meeting of the churches. Upon his return to Denver, Dyer received a letter from the Methodist Conference asking him officially to take charge of the Blue River Mission in Summit County, Colorado Territory. This was a two-week circuit of eight preaching stops high in the mountains along the Continental Divide north of South Park. Until receiving that letter Dyer had not made up his mind to stay in the mountains, but now he accepted the assignment and the next day started on foot for his appointments.

> I crossed the range on a snow path, for although it was April the snow was from five to fifteen feet deep. I reached Georgia Gulch on the second day of April and was received kindly. There were about one hundred and fifty people in the Gulch, and I found some few that had been members of some church. I set preaching for the next Sunday at ten and a half o'clock, and at French Gulch in the afternoon. There was a friendly Jew at Georgia Gulch who proposed to raise the preacher something, and took a paper and collected $22.50 in gold dust, for that was all the currency then. This amount was quite a help, as there were only ten cents in my purse when I got there.

Dyer found a log cabin in French Gulch where he set up his headquarters. Here he described his new home:

*Miner's cabin completely snowed in during a mountain winter.*
Courtesy of Library of Congress Prints and Photographs Division.

The bed was hay, with blankets for covering. I slept well, and rested as well as though I had been in a fine parlor chamber. My furniture was primitive and limited—a table, a couple of boards against the side of the wall for a cupboard, six tin plates, half a set of knives and forks, with a few other things; a coffee pot, a tin cup, and a pot for boiling vegetables—when I could get them—and a frying pan. We cooked by a fireplace, generally baking our bread in a frying pan set up before the fire...I tried to make my cabin useful. It was about eighteen feet square, and was the best place to hold our meetings. The floor was hard ground. I got gunnysacks and made carpet, and covered the table with two copies of the Northwestern Christian Advocate. So I preached to the people in my own house.

With such a transient population in the mining camps, it was almost impossible to establish a church with any longevity, let alone one that could support a regular full-time pastor. Many missionaries complained about this state of affairs, but Dyer developed his own practical solution:

I formed one class and then discovered that there was little profit in it, as the people stopped so short a time in one place. I concluded to get everybody out, and then preach the truth burning hot, whether my hearers were in the house, or around the camp fire, or under the shade of a pine tree. We generally had good congregations. The way we got them out was to go along the gulches and tell the people in their cabins and saloons where the preaching would be at night, and then just before the time, to step to the door where they were at cards and say: "My friends, can't you close your game in ten minutes and come hear preaching?" I tried to adapt myself to the situation, neither showing that I felt above anyone, nor ever compromising with sin or with transgressions, and being ready always to speak for the Lord Jesus Christ.

Dyer never seemed to tire of ministering to people wherever he could gather a crowd, and in almost every case he received good attention and respectful behavior. After preaching to a group in Gibson Gulch, Dyer commented, "Although we all looked rough, the miners treated me and the cause of Christ with respect. Often after preaching I was greeted warmly, and some of them would say the service reminded them of home. They were generally liberal, although it was not the custom always to pass the hat. It was common to give a dollar all around, and to this day I would as soon ask miners for help as any other class of men I have ever found."

Even when conditions were not ideal, Dyer usually came out all right. On one occasion in the settlement near his French Gulch cabin, a large group of men began drinking too much and grew rowdy. They decided that their preacher should either treat the entire group to drinks, or he should give a temperance speech. Here is Dyer's account of the incident:

> It was just daylight when they arrived at my cabin and said: "If you don't open the door we will break it in." I threw it open and invited them in, but they said: "We have come to take you up to Walker's Saloon, and you can either treat or make a temperance speech." Soon there were over forty men, and they called a chairman or moderator, but they were too drunk to be moderated. I got upon a box and said: "Gentlemen, first I will tell you what I think. There is not a man here but would be ashamed for his father, mother, sisters, or brothers to know our condition here this morning." They stamped and roared out: "That is so." I declared, "And next, if we were not so drunk we would not be here now." They cheered: "That's so too!" I wound up and was about to take my leave, but the judge said: "I move that we vote that everything Mr. Dyer has said is true," and they gave a rous-

ing vote. He said, "The ayes have it," and made a motion that they all give Mr. Dyer one dollar apiece, and that was also carried. They took the hat and got twenty dollars, and I thanked them and went home to breakfast.

During the winter it was very difficult to travel through heavy snow to reach his preaching appointments. Dyer decided to make a pair of "snow shoes" for himself—which today would be called snow skis. He used boards that were eight or ten feet long and four or five inches wide, tapering and bending the tips so they would ride above the drifts. It took a great deal of practice to become used to these new "shoes," and Dyer described one outing when he was going down the mountain to Gold Run. "My snow shoes got crossed in front as I was going very fast. A little pine tree was right in my course, and I could not turn and dared not encounter the tree with the shoes crossed, and so I threw myself into the snow and disappeared out of sight."

Every experienced man in the mountains knew that, in order to travel any significant distance, it was best to travel at night when the snow crust was solid. Once the sun touched the slopes, the snow could become soft and unstable. Unfortunately, the hours of darkness were also the time when predatory animals were most active. On one occasion Dyer was to travel over the Continental Divide, where he recorded this incident among the wolves of that region:

*1866 photo of a man using snow-shoes to travel across deep snow.*
Courtesy of Library of Congress Prints and Photographs Division.

About two o'clock in the morning I took my carpet sack, got on my snow shoes, and went up Blue River. The snow was five feet deep and would not bear a man in daytime, even with snow shoes. From about two o'clock until nine or ten in the morning was the only time a man could go, and a horse could not go at all. When about three miles up the Blue River, the wolves set up a tremendous howling quite near. I was not armed, but passed quietly along, and was not disturbed. It was not likely, I thought, that the good Lord would let anything disturb a man going in the night to his appointments, although wolves and bears and mountain lions were numerous. I reached Montgomery about nine o'clock in the morning, and the snow drifted above the tops of the doors.

I had been two years traveling in the Rocky Mountains and had carried no weapons but a pocket knife, and used that mostly to cut shavings and my broiled meat. Some of my friends advised me to arm myself, but I could not see doing it...First, I did not have money to buy a pistol, and in the second place I had been sent there to preach. For two years I had passed all sorts of men, and often slept alone under the shelter of a pine tree when I had reason to believe the mountain lion and the savage bear were my nearest neighbors, and I had never been molested. I felt that I was still in the hands of that same God whom I tried to serve, and that He who had kept me from being a prey to the wild beasts would keep me safe.

On another occasion Dyer was on the top of a mountain just after dusk, searching for the trail in the dim light. He said, "The big owls began to hoo, hoo, and the wolves to howl as if there might be a score of them close by." Dyer was lonely and unsettled, so he started to sing one of his favorite old hymns. As he put it, "I happened to strike the key just right, and the hymn echoed from mountain to mountain and seemed to fill the woods. The owls stopped, and the wolves shut their mouths."

Dyer faithfully ministered across his high mountain circuit during 1863, but as another winter approached the miners began to experience financial struggles. Most of the mining activity depended upon a consistent source of water for washing gold from the surrounding rock, and the cold temperatures would freeze the running water. Here Dyer explains that the situation was becoming increasingly desperate, and yet God's care and timing proved to be perfect for the preacher.

The water failed in many places, and there being some excitement in Idaho and Montana, about one-third of the people left for the bonanzas. What members remained were too poor that they could not get away. This was about the state of the case with the parson. Winter was approaching, and with what little could be expected from the collections and all I had on hand, I had not more than half enough to carry me through. I bought three sacks of flour at fifteen dollars a sack, and had to trust Providence for most of the rest. About mid-winter I found myself without means, and so sought work, but could get none unless I would work on Sundays, which was out of the question.

In the forepart of February a man came to me who had the contract to carry the mail from Buckskin Joe to Cache Creek by California Gulch, a distance of thirty-seven miles. He had carried it as long as he could on a mule. It was once a week, and he offered me eighteen dollars a week to carry it on snow shoes. I thought: "I can preach about as often as I have been doing, and am not obliged to go on Sunday." So I took the mail, and crossed the Mosquito Range every week, and preached three times a week.

The mail's weight was from twenty-three to twenty-six pounds, with from five to seven pounds of express matter. The carriage was on snow shoes, over an Indian trail that was covered from three to twenty feet with snow. My snow shoes were of the Norway style, from nine to eleven feet in length, and ran well when the snow was just right, but were heavy when they gathered snow. I carried a pole to jar the sticking snow off. There was no cabin from Mosquito to California Gulch, and no one living between the Gulch and Cache Creek. I often went at night, as it thawed in the day so that it was impossible to travel. Suffice it to say that the winter of 1863 and 1864 was a remarkably hard one, and the spring held off until June, with terrible snow storms. I was the first to cross the Mosquito Range with a horse, and that was the third day of July.

John Dyer continued to preach throughout his South Park circuit, returning to the towns on the eastern Front Range of the Rockies once a year for the annual meeting of the Methodist Conference. Each minister would receive his assignment at these meetings, and in more ways than one Dyer was now the senior missionary in the region. The Denver district was considered the most desirable, since the preaching locations were closer together, more populated, more accessible, and better funded. Six preachers were appointed to the Denver district that year. The South Park district, however, was spread over hundreds of miles of rugged, inaccessible mountain country with few preachers and non-existent funding. Dyer was reassigned to South Park, along with one other preacher who never reported for his assignment.

Dyer was left alone to cover the territory which included South Park, the Blue River valley to the north, the Arkansas River valley and the region west of the Continental Divide, as well as the Front Range towns of Colorado City, Cañon City, Pueblo, and Trinidad on the New Mexico border. This was far too large a work for one preacher, yet despite his disadvantages, he was determined to include all of southern Colorado, and even northern New Mexico, in his preaching circuit.

# North into Montana

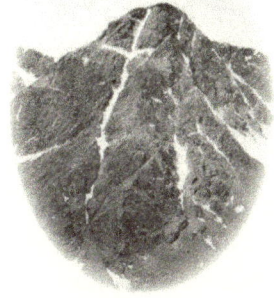

From his vantage point in Colorado, John Dyer had reported that new bonanzas were being discovered to the north in Montana and Idaho. During the final years of the US Civil War, a chain of unusual circumstances eventually led a staunchly southern preacher to the farthest reaches of the West as a missionary.

Methodist minister L.B. Stateler was born and raised in Kentucky, and he was first licensed to preach there in the 1830s. He faithfully ministered to circuits along the Mississippi River, as well as serving at several Indian mission schools across the Midwest. For several years, Stateler had applied to be a missionary with the Flathead Indians, but each time his request had been declined. Eventually he accepted a call to the city of Denver and the nearby mining camps.

Upon his arrival in Denver, Stateler assessed the situation and wrote:

By this time the War between the States was in full blast, and the war feeling was prevalent everywhere. Martial law was the rule in Denver, and it was common for those who arrived there from Missouri, or the border States in particular, to be relieved of whatever weapons they had, although it was known that they were necessary, for protection from Indians or wild beasts, to those crossing the great plains or living out on the frontier away from the city.

*L.B. Stateler,*
*Methodist Minister*

To make matters worse, the church building which Stateler was to occupy had been sold and he was left without a place to live and work. He could see no immediate solution to the problem, so he decided to sell his provisions and return home. He was shocked by a letter from his wife, however, telling him that their home in Kansas had been torched, that everything they owned was in ashes, and that she and their daughter barely escaped with their lives. They warned him not to return, but that they would meet him on the frontier—setting a time to rendezvous at Fort Kearney in Nebraska Territory.

Autumn had turned to winter on the Great Plains, and the Stateler family faced severe storms and biting headwinds on their journey. The prairie was covered with snow for four or five hundred miles, and they were ill-equipped to handle the ferocity of the weather.

> We were poorly prepared, not having a sufficient tent to protect us from the cold at night, nor a good stove on which to cook our food. At first we had fuel, along the Platte River, but soon it gave out, leaving but a vast open waste before us, and nothing in the shape of timber but a fringe of willow brush along the bank. When we came to the last timber, we put all the wood we could haul into the wagon and suspended it with ropes under the axles that it might last as long as possible, not knowing what we would do when it was gone.
>
> Our sufferings during the day were often intense, for we were very poorly clad. We had to use iron pins which were driven in the hard, frozen ground to hold our tent, under which we laid us down on the ground and got what sleep we could. The snow was from six inches to a foot deep, which we would scrape away the best we could to get a place where we could make our beds.
>
> It was one vast, snowy wilderness as far as the eye could reach in every direction. There was not a tree, nor even a hillock, to break the force of the piercing winds that swept the wild, wintry waste. We would travel only a few miles—eight or ten—each day. When we arrived in Denver we had not one dollar, not even a cent, of money to our name.

Upon reaching the settlements, they were little better off than before. They could not return East, and there was nothing for them in Denver. In the meantime, however, gold had been discovered in the northwest—first in the Deer Lodge Valley, then at Bannack City, Grasshopper Creek, and Alder Gulch, where Virginia City was shortly to be built. A new stampede was taking place to the gold fields of Montana. Since they had nothing to lose, the Statelers decided to join the parade. They would be traveling to the country of the Flathead Indians after all. Stateler's biographer described this providential turn of events.

> When he responded to the call to go with the Lees, and later with Whitman to Oregon, his plans were frustrated. After he was thrust out from Kansas and his home destroyed, the church to which he was sent, by a strange procedure, had passed into other hands, and the way was closed against him in Colorado. The Lord had use for him in a new country that he was just preparing, and to which he was now leading him.

A large wagon train was preparing to leave Denver for the Montana country in the spring of 1864, under the leadership of experienced mountaineer Jim Bridger. There were almost three hundred people and sixty-two wagons in the train. They followed the foothills north and made their way across the high prairies of Wyoming. Many river crossings could be forded, but on several occasions they had to build rafts to ferry their provisions across swollen streams.

At this time Indian hostilities were especially intense, and one morning the group discovered that a large village of Indians had made camp during the night within a mile of their position. An attack was expected, since they believed these were members of the hostile Sioux tribe.

Stateler reported what happened next:

> Major Bridger, our captain, went with a small company of unarmed men in the direction of the Indian camp, hoping to obtain an

*Shoshone village in the 1870s, Wyoming Territory.*
Courtesy of Library of Congress Prints and Photographs Division.

47

interview with them. The chief, seeing them approach unarmed, came with a company of his braves in the same manner to meet them. Presently the Indians changed their manner, began to shout "Bridger! Bridger!" at the top of their voices, and came galloping up to where the white men were. They were Shoshone, or Snake, Indians and recognized our captain as their old friend. They had come across the mountains on a buffalo hunt. The chief was a particular friend of Bridger. When we found out who they were and what it all meant, there was great rejoicing. We made them a feast, gave them some presents.

During the course of their journey the members of the wagon train discovered that Stateler was a Methodist minister, and they were determined to have church services as part of their regular routine.

It was soon noised abroad that a preacher was among the emigrants, and without ever speaking a word to me they decided to lay over and not travel on Sunday. From that time on we had regular preaching. There were quite a number of religious people along. The emigrants were civil, respectful, and quiet. We usually camped where there were trees, and the services were held under the shade of those friendly pines. There is something inspiring in such a scene. A company of honest, earnest, liberty-loving, enterprising, well-disposed American citizens, journeying through the trackless wilderness seeking a better country, stopping over each Sabbath day and making the woods and

*1869 sketch of a large wagon train like the one with which the Stateler family traveled.*
Courtesy of Library of Congress Prints and Photographs Division.

mountains echo with their songs of worship and praise to God as they thus halted by the wayside.

On July 8, 1864, toward the end of their journey, they crossed the Madison River. From there Stateler continued two days farther to Virginia City in order to prepare living quarters for his family. He was not able to find a suitable situation, however, so he returned to their camp. The settlement was in transition, so they proceeded to the new diggings at Norwegian Gulch where they pitched their tent on July 20th. They were located about thirty-five miles northeast of Virginia City, and two or three hundred miners were scattered along the creek prospecting for precious minerals.

The Statelers had brought six milk cows and calves with them, and by the time they reached Norwegian Gulch the animals were quite tired and thin. They were allowed to rest and to graze on the rich grass and were soon in good condition again. Since the Statelers had no money, they were relying on their livestock to provide for them.

> An enclosure of pine logs, commonly called a corral, was made in which the calves were kept during the day and the cows at night. The fine grass produced an abundant flow of milk. Milk pans and a tin churn had been brought along, and so were soon supplied with butter. A sparkling mountain stream ran near the tent. A log structure, like an old-fashioned spring house, was built over it in which the milk and butter were kept cool. In addition, a water wheel was soon constructed, by means of which the churn was operated. The butter was sold to the miners for one dollar and a half per pound in gold dust, or three dollars in greenbacks—the prevailing price at the time. During the summer Mrs. Stateler soon made three hundred pounds of butter, which furnished the means to buy the necessaries of life for a time.

Cabins were built of pine logs, with roofs made from poles covered with dirt. The floors were dirt, although some lumber was made using whipsaws. Cooking was typically done at a stone fireplace inside the cabin. Since wild game was still abundant, they were usually supplied with meat. Animal hides were sometimes tanned and used for clothing or to cover handmade furniture.

> Everything in the way of merchandise had to be brought a great distance across the rough mountains, either in wagons or on pack animals. We were more than two hundred miles from Fort Benton,

the head of navigation on the Missouri River, where an occasional steamboat would land a load of supplies from the States. Hence the price for everything was high. The average price of flour was twenty-five dollars a hundredweight in gold, or double that in paper money. It got up to fifty dollars, and even higher, at one time. Coffee was one dollar a pound, and sugar fifty cents. Coarse blankets sold for twenty dollars a pair in gold, while common calicoes and coarse plain goods were fifty cents a yard in gold, or a dollar in greenbacks, and everything else was in proportion. An ordinary cook stove was worth two hundred and fifty dollars.

Early in the winter of 1864 a heavy snow fell, and the supply wagons coming from Salt Lake were not able to reach the northern mining camps. This created a high demand for the limited stock of provisions, so stores sold their goods at exorbitant prices. Stateler reported that "this caused much suffering among the people, and for a while our missionaries had to live on meat straight, and wild meat at that, such as could be killed in the mountains where the snow was deep in midwinter or early spring, and which, of course, was not of the best quality."

In Norwegian Gulch, Stateler found several families who were eager for church services, as well as another minister named Hardgrove who had come from Missouri to work the gold fields.

> Almost the first thing after getting settled was to prepare a place for preaching, which we did by erecting an arbor made of forks set in the ground on which poles were laid and covered with brush. The people were elated at the idea of having preaching, joined heartily in the work, and most of the miners ceased work on Sunday that they might come to church. The attendance was good, and many took an active part, especially in the singing. The two preachers, Stateler and Hardgrove, alternated each Sunday morning and afternoon.

When Stateler visited Virginia City he had made the acquaintance of several Methodists and other church-goers. These people said, "We have no minister, and we want you to come and preach for us." They began building a large log structure in town which came to be known as the "Log Church," containing seats and benches for those who would attend. When this building was finished, Major J.R. Boyce wrote to Stateler and invited him to come preach for them.

> I mounted my horse and rode over at once and began preaching. This was about the first of February, and the appointments were kept

for four months, traveling two hundred miles over the rough mountain roads through the cold and snow, crossing two mountain ranges each way. The attendance at church was large, the people attentive and liberally disposed, for gold was plentiful in every man's pocket. Although the preacher was poor and hardly able to afford the necessities of life, yet he did not receive enough to pay his horse fare at the livery stable—simply because the preacher was too modest to take a collection for himself.

When most of the miners left Norwegian Gulch for the winter, Stateler moved his camp about fifteen miles to the Jefferson Valley where there was less snow and the grazing was better for his livestock. Later Stateler began preaching at Willow Creek, which was only a few miles from his new headquarters. He gave his first sermon there on Christmas Day at the cabin of a Mr. Nave. This became part of Stateler's regular circuit in that area, where he preached in the larger cabins and organized the first official Methodist Episcopal Church in Montana.

It was not intended to be permanent. In fact, there was nothing regarded as permanent in the country at that time. It was not considered a desirable place to live in. Those who had come to dig gold expected to go elsewhere to enjoy their prospective fortunes, and most of those who had come to find refuge from the storm of war expected to return to their homes when the war cloud had passed away.

While many would come and go, L.B. Stateler was one who remained. His "accidental" ministry in Montana was to last for over thirty years. He traveled thousands of miles, experienced incredible hardships, and subsisted for years without help from a mission board or salary from his parishioners. He was one of that rare breed of missionaries who sacrificed everything he had in order to fulfill his calling, even though he had been led to it by tragic circumstances, with no funds to rely on except his own resources and God's provision.

# South into New Mexico

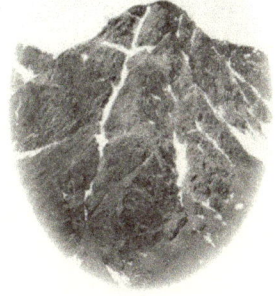

In a previous chapter we learned that Methodist preacher John Dyer had been appointed to cover all of southern Colorado Territory in 1865. He was interested in reaching farther south into New Mexico Territory as well. Since the high mountain districts were snowed in, Dyer determined to travel along the foothills into the southern portion of his new circuit.

This was the latter part of March, 1865, and the mountains were almost impassable. Accordingly, I left Pueblo for Captain Craig's Ranch, twenty miles south on the road to Trinidad. Next day I wished to go through, but it snowed hard and the roads were heavy. At the Pishapah Creek it was dark. I could not see the road, had nothing for the pony, so I hitched up for the night, gathered some dead brush, built a small fire, sat on the saddle, and covered up with the saddle blanket. It snowed till it was nine inches deep. It was a good time to reflect, for it was next to impossible to sleep. Daylight came at last. I started on, but such a snow to ball up on the horse's feet has not often been seen. At eleven, reached Mr. Gray's ranch and was kindly taken in and cared for. Next day, Sunday, with his consent I gathered in some neighbors and preached to about thirty. It continued so rough that I stayed till Tuesday morning, and went two miles to Trinidad. I stopped overnight and talked to them who could speak English.

While in southern Colorado, Dyer visited several people with experience in New Mexico Territory. From these conversations Dyer became convinced that the regions to the south could benefit from the ministry of Protestant missionaries. He determined to go, and he found two traveling companions who knew the Spanish language.

> From those who had traveled there, I was led to feel that they ought to have the gospel in New Mexico, and now as I had the opportunity I concluded to extend my district so as to include that country. The next day, with two gentlemen, I crossed the Raton Mountain...We saw the tracks of two footmen in the snow, and soon met some folks who told us the footmen were a Mexican man and woman running off to get married. I told my companions that I could marry them, and one of the men rode on to overtake them. We came to the foot of the mountain where he had corralled them on a bare spot of ground. All things being ready, and my companion acting as interpreter, I went through with the ceremony and wished the couple much happiness. The groom took my hand and kissed it on the back, and handed it to the bride and she kissed it too. I wrote out a certificate in full, stating my residence and church, and my interpreter translated it into Spanish with the names of the witnesses. They asked what was the charge. It was no time to make charges, and I told them I never charged poor people for anything.

Dyer's first ministerial act in this new region had been to perform an unexpected marriage in a snowy valley in the wilderness. This was a fitting start for his missionary exploration of New Mexico. Dyer was following the Mountain Route of the Santa Fe Trail, and this road led him toward the southwest along the foothills of the Sangre de Cristo range to the village of Cimarron. Lucien Maxwell was the owner of a vast Mexican land grant, and the headquarters of his empire was located at Cimarron.

> The next place of note was Maxwell's. He had a large house and ranch, surrounded by Mexicans and Indians. I stayed with him overnight, I was treated well, and entertained free of charge. Got some information as to the settlements. He told me there were several families down the Cimarron Creek and advised me to visit them, as they were Americans. It was Sunday morning. I rode seven miles and collected about twenty-five people and preached to them. This was the first Protestant service ever held on the now famous Maxwell Land Grant.

From there Dyer continued south to Las Vegas, New Mexico, where he preached to a few English-speaking people. He finally reached Santa Fe and located a Baptist minister who was probably the only other Protestant preacher in New Mexico Territory at that time. The following Sunday they gathered about forty people for services. Afterward, Dyer turned north toward Taos, Red River, and his return to Colorado. Within a month the Baptist minister had returned East to his home, leaving New Mexico without a Protestant preacher.

By June 1865 Dyer had reached Denver where he attended the annual Methodist Conference. While there he shared about his explorations in New Mexico, and he urged the leaders to send a qualified preacher to that region—an educated man who could speak Spanish and endure hardships. Unfortunately, no such man could be found, but Dyer would not give up. Three years later at the Methodist annual meeting, Dyer created a map of the "Colorado Conference" which included all of New Mexico and the southern portion of Wyoming. He did everything he could to convince the conference leaders that missionaries were needed in New Mexico. When the assignments were read at the end of that session, John L. Dyer had been assigned to go alone into New Mexico.

Dyer was shocked by this appointment, since he considered himself unqualified for the ministry there. "The thought of going there rather set me back. I felt my inability to do what ought to be done in that mission." Dyer urged the leaders to send an educated man who knew the Spanish language, but they replied, "You preach to all the Americans, and do what you can to see where the Mexicans can be improved."

Dyer accepted the assignment and wrote, "This appointment was not taken without at least some knowledge of the labor, privation, and dangers attending a Protestant preacher in that field...It may have been for the best to take a man who was used to mountain life, who could ride a pony on an Indian trail, and feared nothing when convinced that he was right."

Packing his few belongings, Dyer traveled out of South Park across Poncha Pass and into the San Luis Valley. On the second day he camped near Fort Garland and gathered about a dozen people there for preaching. Entering New Mexico, Dyer journeyed for another two days in order to reach a new mining camp in the Baldy country just west of Cimarron.

*Elizabethtown, New Mexico, in the early 1870s.*
Courtesy of Old Mill Museum.

I reached Elizabethtown, a mining camp of several hundred, mostly Americans. Here I made my headquarters for the year. I held a meeting for two weeks; had one member to help—Brother Simon Tyrer. I had preached at his house in Wisconsin in 1851. At the close of the meeting, seven others joined. This was the first class that I know of in New Mexico. This year I preached at Trinidad, Red River, Cimarron, Taos, Mora, Tipton, Watrous, and Cherry Valley. Early in the spring I went to Santa Fe, Las Vegas, and Tuckalota.

At Santa Fe, Dyer found a Presbyterian preacher named McFarland, who had just established a small congregation. Dyer stayed for two weeks to help him with the teaching and preaching, saying, "I advised all to join his church. He thought there were about twenty-five converts." Denominational rivalry had not yet reached the West!

During his explorations Dyer determined that the best location for a church and school would be in La Junta, located northeast of Las Vegas, New Mexico. From his years of ministry in Wisconsin, Dyer also knew a young preacher with the required education and experience. He wrote to Thomas and Emily Harwood, asking them to take charge of this new work. At first they declined, and Dyer was very concerned that no qualified preacher could be found. A few months later Dyer contacted the Harwoods again. Here Dyer describes this providential series of events.

Bishop Ames failed to find a man, and I was in great anxiety, with constant prayer to God for help. I took down a coat that had hung by the wall for months, and found an old letter from Brother Harwood, saying he could not come. But as I looked it over, it seemed to me that if I would write again, he might change his mind. I did so, and received the welcome news that he would come.

As Dyer waited for the Harwoods to move to New Mexico, he made his headquarters in Santa Fe and from there traveled across most of the Territory. He followed the Rio Grande Valley and preached in Albuquerque, Socorro, Fort Craig, Fort Selden, Las Cruces, El Paso, and all points in between.

At Lone Rocks, twenty miles above Fort Selden, the company spread tent-cloths over two wagons, and I tried to preach to them in that desert place, the very spot where the Indians at various times had leaped out from behind the rocks and scalped the weary traveler... After prayer an old Mexican took my hand and said he could not understand English, but he knew my preaching was in the right way... At Fort Stanton I found a man who was living with a woman with a contract that they should be married as soon as they could get a preacher to tie the knot. I married them, and the groom gave me ten dollars. After preaching to a large turn-out, one of the captains got up an extra good dinner and invited me to dine with several of the officers. Next day I started for Ashland. I stopped at a grist mill and preached to eight Americans and two Mexicans. For fear of Indians, they locked my horse in the mill, and barred the doors of the cabin... Reached Ashland without trouble. Here they seemed glad to hear a sermon. Word was sent around and a mixed congregation of forty-five came together. At the close, a collector stood at the door and received gifts to the amount of thirteen dollars for me.

Dyer returned to La Junta to await the arrival of Thomas Harwood on the stagecoach. Harwood had left his wife, Emily, with relatives in the East and came alone in order to make living arrangements for them. Here Harwood describes his arrival after midnight when the stagecoach finally reached La Junta, later called Tiptonville:

When the stage halted in front of the store of Col. W.B. Tipton, I soon heard a familiar voice from the only man in all New Mexico whom I knew at that time, saying: "Come out of there Brother Harwood, I know you are there." It was my old friend and brother in the ministry, Father Dyer. He and Col. Tipton had set up until past midnight waiting for the arrival of the stage. They both seemed delighted to see me...It had been a long, cold, tedious journey, and to say that

I was tired did not half express it; so I retired as soon as they would let me, but was up quite early next morning to look out upon a part of what was to be my parish.

We lost no time. We secured another horse and rode over the country up and down the valleys of the Mora and Sapello Rivers, visiting all the Americans we could find and some natives, and while they were the most mixed people, politically, religiously, morally and socially with whom I had ever met, they treated us nicely and seemed glad to see us and to have us pray in their families, and to know that we were going to establish schools and preaching appointments among them...The people not only seemed glad to see us, but often insisted strongly for us to pass the night with them, and almost without exception invited us to hold religious services with them.

As Father Dyer was soon to leave for Santa Fe, I asked him to give me the metes and bounds of my circuit. Father Dyer replied: "Start out northward via Fort Union, Ocate, Elizabethtown, Cimarron, Vermejo and Red River until you meet a Methodist preacher coming this way, then come back on some other road and rest up a little; thence go south via Las Vegas, etc., until you meet other Methodist preachers coming this way. All this will be your work."

*Methodist Minister, Thomas Harwood*

Since Harwood was the only Methodist preacher in the entire Territory, his work would be large indeed. After his short tour of northern New Mexico with Harwood, John Dyer returned to Colorado for a new preaching assignment, having traveled a little over ten thousand miles on horseback during his two years in New Mexico. Harwood was left alone to conduct the ministry in this vast territory. He set out on his first solo trip on the northern circuit, and here he describes some of his adventures:

I left Tiptonville, New Mexico, on November 12, 1869, for Ocate by way of Fort Union, and passed the night at the house of the Hon. Charles Williams, thence over a spur of the Rocky Mountains toward Black Lakes...I saw the finest meteor I had ever seen. It looked as large as the moon right in daylight. It was almost as bright as the sun. It seemed so near, I wondered why I did not hear it strike the earth. I galloped across the prairie, half a mile or more, looking for it.

I expected it would set the prairie afire. I spent several hours, I think, but found no traces of it. I spent so much time looking for the meteor it was getting late when I got up among the foothills, the trails being very poorly traveled, and began to fear that I might not be able to make Black Lakes before dark, and as the Indians, wolves and mountain lions were very common and dangerous, I began to think of turning back and spending the night with my old friend again.

I reached Black Lakes just before sunset. There was only one house in sight at the Lakes, and only one room and two or three families, seventeen in all, occupying it. I preached that night to sixteen people, as one was absent. The next day I took dinner at a house at a point where the roads forked, one to Taos and the other to Elizabethtown. The man was an American with a Mexican family. I had some thought of staying the night as I was very tired, but the man seemed too friendly and so anxious for me to stay that I began to mistrust that he was not all right. They told me at Elizabethtown that it was well I did not pass the night there, that quite a few had stopped there and had never been heard from since. Time passed and the same man got into trouble and was lynched...I inquired who it was, and learned it was the man at whose house I came near spending the night on that first trip to Elizabethtown. They took up the floor and dug under his cabin, finding the bodies of three men that had been buried there.

In Elizabethtown I preached on Sunday the 14th of November, both morning and night, to small congregations...Next day came six miles down to Mr. Pascoe's where I spent the night, with religious services. It was a very large family. A widower with a large number of children, and a widow with about the same number had been married back East, and were raising quite a number of younger ones, and they were all girls and too numerous to count...I also visited Willow Creek, close to Elizabethtown, thence down to Cimarron, where I spent the night at a hotel.

I also found a Mr. Rinehart, whose wife had been a member of our church back in Pennsylvania...The seventeenth went on as far as Red River Station. It was a cold day and one of the windiest I had ever experienced. I met with the same generous hospitality that I had met at La Junta and Cimarron. Supper, lodging, breakfast and horse feed and no charge...The eighteenth was Thanksgiving Day, and thirty miles over the Raton Divide brought me to Trinidad where I expected to meet Mrs. Harwood, who had been left at Kansas City to visit some friends. The midnight stage arrived, but Mrs. Harwood was not with it.

I went down to Rev. E.J. Rice's house, whose acquaintance I made on my way down, to visit them and to attend their prayer meeting. I met Mr. Rice who took me into another room, and pretty soon some ladies came to the prayer meeting. Mr. Rice said there would be no prayer meeting as Mrs. Rice was about to be sick. The next day I learned that a boy baby had been born, who was named after his father. We could hardly expect him to be as good a man as his father, though, since the first act of his life was to break up a prayer meeting!

Two days' waiting did not bring Mrs. Harwood. The train from Kansas City to its terminus at Sheridan, Kansas, had failed to make time. I had my work laid out for me the approaching Sunday, so had to leave for Vermejo so as to be there Saturday night...I preached at Cimarroncito Sunday morning at 10 o'clock and at 2:30 at Sweetwater and at Ocate at night, making forty-five miles and three sermons that day. Mrs Harwood arrived the next day on the stage at about midnight at Tiptonville.

When I reached home I found I had traveled about four hundred miles, and preached eleven times to sixty-eight people. I said to Mrs. Harwood, "If we had remained in Wisconsin I could have had an appreciative congregation of perhaps two to three hundred people without the four hundred miles horseback ride or the efforts to gather the people together for worship."

I had a little tinge of homesickness. I could not help asking myself, "Why am I here? What can I do?" A hundred thousand people whose language, religion and customs are just as foreign as if they were in a foreign land. But I started by trusting in Him who hath said, "Lo, I am with thee always unto the end of the world."

The residents of the area were delighted to welcome the Harwoods, especially since they intended to establish a church and school. Harwood commented, "They seemed to be much more concerned about the school than about the preaching, as they had been anticipating my wife's arrival for some time." In La Junta the Harwoods were not able to find a suitable house in which to live, but a family in nearby Cherry Valley invited them to use one of their buildings as a residence.

There was also an adobe chicken coop on the property, and the owner turned the chickens out, cleaned up the floor, and whitewashed

*Methodist Church
in Tiptonville, New
Mexico, dedicated
by the Harwoods in
1870.*
Reprinted from Harwood
(1908), Vol 1, 373.

the interior as a place for the school to meet. The next day school was opened with about thirty students, and two weeks later a Sunday School was organized and preaching services were held there. Years later the question was raised as to who opened the first Sunday School in New Mexico. Harwood wrote, "We think we were the first. At any rate we think we have the right to *crow* as ours was opened in a *hen-house*."

Harwood's circuit in northeastern New Mexico included the stagecoach stops of Red River, Crow Creek, and Vermejo. He preached there for several years, and the people appreciated his regular visits.

> There was a stage station at each place and a kind of headquarters for cattle men. The people always treated me well and called me "Parson." I was up on the Vermejo, so close to the Raton mountain range, riding up and down the valley announcing the preaching appointment for the evening, breathing the mixture of the plains and mountain pure air, feeling perhaps that I was the monarch of all I surveyed, as there was no other preacher for miles.

Elizabethtown became the county seat of the newly-created Colfax County, New Mexico, and in those days it had more than a thousand residents. It had been John Dyer's first headquarters when he opened the territory for the Methodists, and Harwood was able to dedicate the first Methodist church building in Elizabethtown soon after his arrival in the Territory. Here Harwood describes its beautiful setting:

> The town is situated in the midst of the finest mountain scenery I ever saw, among some beautiful little hills which seem to have rolled

down from the huge mountain above. In front of the village is a little valley sloping from the east and west, through which runs a beautiful little mountain stream. Beyond the valley rises up in majestic grandeur "Bald Mountain," said to be the highest of all the southern chain. Rev. J.L. Dyer and myself took the summer trail and crossed over "Old Baldy," as it is here called. We started on our ponies, winding our way up through gulches and canyons, and at length reached the foot of the immediate mountain, where we found gold diggings and a family residing. Here we rested and took dinner. Being much refreshed we journeyed on, leading our ponies most of the way, now and then stopping to blow, for the mountain air is so rarefied that one who is not used to it will soon be out of breath.

The little fir trees with which the north side of the mountain is lined all sparkling with their pure white frosty dresses, and the hazy distance below us, with the light, fleecy clouds kissing the mountain sides were scenes of beauty grand beyond description. A few struggles more and we reached the top. There we stood 2½ miles higher than we were when in our boyhood days we had climbed up in the highest treetops on the Atlantic coast. Soon the frosty air made us feel like seeking a warmer clime and we descended on the south side into a canyon where two quartz mills were grinding out gold. We gathered a congregation and Father Dyer preached.

We spent a little time in one of the deepest canyons looking at the stars in the daytime. I knew about where in the sky to look for Venus, and I think Jupiter, and had no trouble seeing them, which seemed quite a novel thing to Father Dyer. We also spent some time in amusing ourselves in measuring the high cliffs in the rocks by means of a pole and its shadow and the height of some of the high points.

Harwood was fascinated with the natural world around him, and New Mexico certainly contained a large number of interesting natural phenomena to investigate. On one occasion Harwood had an exciting encounter with a tarantula while he was traveling toward Santa Fe:

On the road to Santa Fe, I was a mile or so ahead of the freight teams and found a tarantula crossing the road just ahead of me. It was the largest I had or have ever seen. With a small branch broken off a pine I was trying to hold it until the teams came up, but the thing didn't like to be held and would start off from me. I struck down in front of it a few times to stop it, but the last time it sprang at me and came near striking me in the face. It scared me worse than when the Rebs would come at us with their bayonets in the war. Neither Webster nor the Universal Dictionary does justice to the tarantula in their description of it. The Universal Dictionary says they are about an inch long. This was much larger than that. Its legs must have been three or four inches long, and its body all of three or four, I would think. It is evident these authors have never seen our Southwest tarantula. I slept securely out on the ground until I encountered that thing. After that I begged a bed in one of the big wagons and felt much safer, even if that bed was a little hard.

As Harwood expanded his New Mexico ministry he was able to bring others along to assist with the efforts. Soon Elizabethtown was able to support a full-time pastor, and N.S. Buckner was appointed to that post. Harwood escorted the Buckners from the annual conference in Denver to their new post in New Mexico, and here Harwood describes a narrow escape they experienced on their journey:

As we were returning from the Colorado Conference, held in Denver, we met with a memorable accident. Rev. N.S. Buckner and wife were in company with me, on their way to their new appointment at Elizabethtown. We had been on the road six days, had traveled about three hundred miles, and were within a day's travel of their destination, when about four miles out of Cimarron, a little before sunset we encountered a terrific thunder storm. The lightning struck our buggy and probably ran down the steel springs that held the top up, tore two great holes in the ground right under the buggy, broke the whiffletrees, knocked the horses down, and for some time badly shocked and paralyzed all of us. Mrs. B. was sitting on the right side of the buggy, I on the left, and brother B. in the middle, driving. I remember the flash of lightning, the terrible crash of thunder, a kind of sulphuric odor, the falling of the horses, and a peculiar deathlike sensation that ran through my system, and there was a short pause of insensibility. We were all badly hurt, but the effects seemed different upon each. I was severely stunned and paralyzed, and lay on the roadside in a drenching shower several minutes unable to speak. I knew what I wanted to say, but terms and names were gone. I could not think of Bro. Buckner's name so as to speak it. Sister B. was worse hurt than any of us, and seemed for a moment to be helpless, chained to the buggy seat. Sister B. and I rolled out of the buggy somehow while he was crying to her, "hold on and I will help you out," and could scarcely move a muscle himself. While lying on the ground so helpless, much of my life passed before me in quick review.

While Bro. B. was not hurt as badly as either of us, I think his sufferings were greater. I had to weep when I saw him lay her down with a tearful kiss commending her to God, and then ran for the horses that were frantically staggering away across the prairie, for it occurred to him we must have a doctor and would better get the horses while they were in reach. How I wanted to tell him that she would soon be better, but my power of speech was yet in a mysterious jumble. As soon as we were able to walk, we left the horses and buggy, and under the blazing lightnings and almost deafening thunder, muddy, wet and barefoot, we made our way three miles to the nearest house, and thence in a wagon to Cimarron. The next day we took the stage for Elizabethtown, where we spent the Sabbath in our neat little church building, Bro. B. preaching in the morning and I at night, and both feeling deeply impressed with the greatness and goodness of God.

Harwood later reported that the original church in Elizabethtown served its purpose for preaching and Sunday School services for several years, but that it was eventually blown down during a severe wind storm and was crushed to splinters. Thomas and Emily Harwood were to spend the rest of their long and productive lives ministering together in New Mexico.

# A Diversity of Preachers

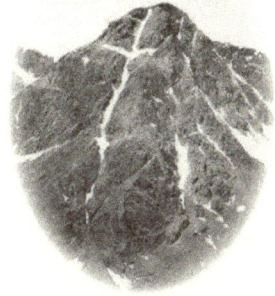

A s we have seen, it was typical for the Methodist preachers to arrive first in many new frontier settlements. An old story tells of a Presbyterian minister who got very excited when he noticed he was the only preacher on the first train into a new area. He thought he would finally be able to beat the Methodists to start the first church in the region. When he arrived at the station and walked into town, though, he saw a Methodist preacher already staking out the lot where he would build his church. When the Presbyterian asked the Methodist how he arrived first, the man said, "Well, I rode on the cow-catcher and jumped off while the train was pulling into station!"

Other Protestant denominations were also sending home missionaries into the frontier settlements about this time. In 1863 the Congregationalists sent William Crawford to serve as the pastor of their new church in Central City, Colorado. In 1865 George M. Randall, an Episcopal bishop, arrived in Denver.

Randall had been commissioned in Boston as the "Missionary Bishop of Colorado and Parts Adjacent." This jurisdiction originally included the territories of

*Men riding the cow catcher on front of a steam locomotive.*

George M. Randall,
Episcopal Minister

Colorado, Idaho, Montana, and Wyoming, but a year later New Mexico was added and Montana and Idaho were removed. When he arrived in the region Randall traveled to Golden where he established the first Episcopal church there. He also was concerned for the education of the children in the region, and he especially noted the lack of opportunities for higher education in the territory. To remedy this situation, Randall was instrumental in founding the Colorado University Schools, based in Jarvis Hall, which included a mining school that later became the Colorado School of Mines.

During his first five years on the frontier, Randall established many other churches and schools, such as St. Mark's Academy in Cheyenne, Wyoming, and St. Peter's Institute in Pueblo, Colorado. He also explored and sent missionaries to New Mexico, for which he gives the following report:

> The majority of Americans there prefer our services to any other. Some have been attached to them at home. Others have been in the army, and are partial to a liturgy. The native population have been accustomed to a liturgical worship, and they have always seen the ministers of God clad in clerical vestments when officiating in public worship. I need not here point out the advantages which our Church possesses over other religious bodies in these particulars; with her bishops, priests, and deacons, with her time-honored liturgy, with the order and impressive solemnity of her worship.

During his ministry in the mountains Randall traveled throughout the Territories of Wyoming, Colorado, and New Mexico—wherever a stagecoach could carry him. Here he outlines his strategy for planting churches in as many places as possible:

> My plan is to dot this jurisdiction all over with consecrated places of worship. In order to do this, they must necessarily be small and inexpensive; cheap, only in cost, not in appearance. Proper proportions cost nothing. To lay a brick, or saw and nail a board, in a way that produces a legitimate and pleasing effect, costs no more than to do these things in a way which is only ugly and misshapen. The building of cheap churches, in such a manner that the House of God shall never be mistaken for any other house, is something of an art. I have made this a matter of study, until I am prepared to say that, in

this country where material and labor are at high prices, a church in Gothic style, twenty feet by forty, with an open timber roof, pointed windows of stained glass, a triplet window in the chancel, bell turret, porch, and comfortable pews, can be built for fifteen hundred dollars!

Randall established several dozen churches, missionary stations, and almost a dozen schools in the growing settlements along the frontier. He was especially effective in appealing to his eastern constituents for missionary funds to establish Episcopal institutions in the West. George Randall would die from pneumonia in 1873 at his home in Denver, but in 1867 Randall had returned to New York to give the dedication speech for a young minister who was being commissioned as a missionary bishop. After seminary graduation, Daniel S. Tuttle came to assist the elderly rector of a small congregation in rural New York. While attending the annual church convention in New York City, Tuttle was nominated as a missionary and the following year was commissioned to the new post of Missionary Bishop in Montana.

On June 3, 1867, Daniel Tuttle took the train to the end of the line in North Platte, Nebraska. He had never been outside his home state of New York. The stagecoach had been delayed at North Platte because of Indian attacks along the trail ahead. Here Tuttle describes his thoughts as he began this new adventure:

Evidently it was virgin soil which I was sent to till. No clergyman of our church had even so much as set foot in Montana...They were days of strange experience to me. I had never before been west of my native state of New York. Now I was at the terminus of all railway travel and the limit of civilization. I had never seen Indians, save a few peaceful Tuscaroras at Niagara Falls, but now the plains all round me were inhabited by thousands of these hostile men. Emigrant wagons and ox-trains and mule-trains before this were quite unknown to me, and such things with their accessories filled North Platte to the full. The tents and flags, the uniforms and accoutrements of the United States military service presented in the encampment yonder were also new to me, for though four years of Civil War had been lately raging, my lot had been cast in scenes remote from that activity. Only thirty years old, I was by no means an especially brave man but rather naturally inclined to be prudent and shrinking, with such a non-belligerent bodyguard as two clergymen and two young women, for whose safety indeed I was to be largely responsible...I have been out and purchased two rifles for Mr. Goddard and myself, at twenty-seven dollars each. This afternoon we shall go out and practice shooting with them. The party starting out tomorrow will consist of more than twenty cool, strong, well-armed men, besides ourselves, most of them Westerners familiar with the plains and living in Denver. If we were not to go now with this strong party we might not have as good a chance later.

Tuttle traveled with a well-armed party, and within a few days reached Denver without incident. While waiting in that city for severe weather in the mountains to clear, Tuttle attended a church meeting with fifty or more people. He was impressed by the intelligent conversation, as well as the directness and lack of pretense among the people. He commented, "They are very little impressed by dignitaries. We two bishops attracted very little attention. At least I did, very little. All were civil, courteous and polite. But there was a self-respect which allowed none of them to attempt any flattery." This was Tuttle's first experience with frontier character, and he appreciated what he saw.

The stagecoach between Denver and Salt Lake City took the northern route through Wyoming Territory. When they reached Fort Bridger they noticed a nearby Shoshone Indian village of sixty or seventy teepees. At the fort they met an older gentleman named Judge Carter, who invited them to tea. Tuttle asked whether there were any Sunday services at Fort Bridger, and Mrs. Carter said, "I have been here six years, and in that time have heard but two sermons." The judge said, "I marry and bury, using the Prayer-Book service for burying." Tuttle promised that he would try to send them a missionary, and if he couldn't find someone, then he would preach to them himself.

After his arrival in Salt Lake City, he took the stagecoach north into the Territory of Idaho. The Snake River was nearly at flood stage and it took a great deal of courage and ingenuity to cross, but after-

*Daniel S. Tuttle,*
*Episcopal Minister*

ward they climbed steadily east until reaching the summit of the Continental Divide. From there they descended into Montana Territory accompanied by a cold rain. After spending the night at the Beaverhead Cañon stage station, they opened the door in the morning to see snow on the ground. Tuttle wrote, "Two inches of snow were lying on the earth, and this was the morning of the 18th of July!" His traveling companion made a discouraging remark, but Tuttle replied, "Montana pleases me more than the other territories for these two special reasons. First, there are trees here, many of the mountains and nearly all the ravines being plentifully covered with mountain pine. Secondly, there are plenty of living springs and streams of water, the freshest, coolest, purest, and sweetest in the world."

They arrived safely in Virginia City after a journey of over 450 miles from Salt Lake City. Tuttle quickly discovered that he had brought an inferior form of money to purchase his provisions.

> The usual currency in all stores here is gold dust. Every little shop has its pair of balances and takes dust in return for goods, at eighteen dollars an ounce. Some dust is worth more, some less, but in buying and selling at stores this is the standard. At the banks they have tests for the dust, and will pay only its intrinsic worth, as tested. Dust here, as compared with greenbacks, is at a fifteen percent premium. For instance, I went to a store and bought a hat. The price was $8, or $9.20 in greenbacks. Every man carries a little buckskin pouch, and in that his money, that is, gold dust. There is a nugget here in the bank, found a few days ago, of solid gold worth about $420. It weighs nearly two pounds.

Tuttle and his traveling companion took a room at the Planters' House Hotel, one of the few wood frame buildings in town. Their room was about twelve feet square, with one double and two single beds. "Mr. G. and I occupy the double. As there is need, the landlord sends whom he will to the cots. No lock is on the door, no wash bowl or pitcher in the room. Every morning we go down to the office to wash, wiping our faces on the office towel." He found the cool nights delightful for sleeping.

Tuttle remained in Virginia City for three weeks, holding services in the upper floor of a large log building which was called the "council chamber" because it housed a branch of the Territorial Legislature. One Sunday Tuttle penned these words in a letter to his wife:

> Anything but Sunday seems this to me, as I sit down and hear feet moving, chains clanking, teamsters shouting more noisily than other days (because the miners from the gulches all round come in today). A stalwart man, ringing a large hand bell, is shouting in front of this hotel. "Now, gentlemen, now's your chance. There's a large stock of goods to be sold just below, in Bridge Street, consisting of miners' equipment, picks, shovels, dry goods of all kinds, and mountain trout and salmon, etc., etc. Sure sale, gentlemen, a man has left the

stock to be cleaned out at auction, whether he gets two cents for it or not; now's your chance, gentlemen." A half dozen teamsters are yelling together, like demons, at their oxen. Indeed, anything but a calm, quiet Sunday is this. Before breakfast I went up to the post office and out of the one or two hundred stores along the streets only a solitary one was closed. That was the First National Bank. Last evening there was a Democratic meeting in front of this hotel, and the speakers were on the balcony just outside of our window. It was sickening to see them drink whiskey and hear the profanity and blasphemy of their talk, as by twos and threes the speakers would retire into the room just adjoining us. I feel sad for the country's future. O Father above, in mercy guide and rule our rulers; in mercy, in Thy purity and power, save our country.

This proved to Tuttle that there was an obvious need for his ministry on this new frontier. Later he wrote these thoughts to his wife, who had remained in New York with their infant son:

In spite of all the drawbacks of this town, its cold, its roughness, its log cabins, you and I, if it be God's will for us to live and work here, could be very happy. Kind hearts are here, cultivated women are here, intelligent society is here, some children are here, and such a field for immediate faithful Church work as I never before saw.

Part of his reason for concluding they could be happy in Montana had to do with the stunning natural beauty of the place. Tuttle said:

I can't describe to you the beauties and grandeurs to be seen here. I hope one day you will see them. Think of long, high ranges, stretching hundreds of miles away, with snow on the tops and sides, the peaks bare and bald, many of the slopes wooded, billows on billows, by the thousand, of hills between the ranges, green valleys with streams, deep gorges and cañons. Think of them all and arrange them in mental prospect in the most grand and beautiful ways, and you have the views we saw yesterday.

Soon afterward Tuttle moved into a log cabin owned by the printer of the *Montana Post* newspaper. This one-room cabin, sixteen feet by twenty-four feet in size, contained only two beds and a few other essentials, but it was far superior to the hotel as a headquarters. After planning for his work in the Territory, Tuttle traveled one hundred twenty-five miles to Helena, another prominent mining camp. He described it as "a town of about four thousand inhabitants, pitched, as you might expect, in the bottom of a dirty mining gulch." He held services there and then planned a long preaching circuit to Fort Bridger, Salt Lake City, and Idaho before returning to his headquarters in Virginia City.

The distances to be traveled by an itinerant minister were immense. Tuttle received a letter from a friend in Boise, Idaho, which told of a visiting English clergyman, Mr. Pope, whom Tuttle had met at Salt Lake City. His friend wrote, "He proposed a *little* walk, and we started out and went up through Oregon into Washington, around into Montana, down through Dakota, Colorado, Arizona, and up through Nevada to home." Here Tuttle describes his lengthy journey into Wyoming, Utah, and Idaho:

I left Virginia City to make my first visit in Idaho. A day or two after I left, poor Mrs. Donaldson died. I went direct to Salt Lake and then eastward on the Overland stage to pay my promised visit to Fort Bridger. I spent Sunday there, the guest of Judge Carter, holding services morning and evening in the Post Hospital. These were the first of our religious services ever held there. Subsequently, by a survey ordered to settle the doubtful line, Fort Bridger, which had been counted in Utah, was adjudged to belong to Wyoming. This, therefore, was the last as well as the first of my services at this post.

I preach in log cabins. I sleep on blankets, sheets being unknown things. I am the guest of bachelors in their dirt-roofed mansions. I travel by stage, on horseback, afoot. I am moving about almost constantly. I have gone about five hundred miles, and have twelve hundred more immediately before me.

Sunday, October 6th, I spent in Salt Lake, then on the 9th I took stage for Boise City, a distance of four hundred miles, the fare for which was $120. The road is more solitary than any in Montana. For hundreds of miles you see no vestige of civilized man except the stations and the stock-tenders kept by the stage company. I arrived at Boise on Saturday afternoon, with broken neck, bruised head, aching bones, sore throat, and disturbed temper.

We left Boise and arrived here [Idaho City], the road being one of the wildest and roughest I have been on. Fortunately it is free from Indians. Steep hills up and down, dug-ways along ravine sides, and narrow trails in cañons barely wide enough for the stage to pass through. It's a queer place in which I write this—the law office of Col. Samuel A. Merritt, a Virginian who was a rebel officer in the late war. Through the thin partition on the right I hear the tramping and talking of men coming and going in the post office, which is also a stationery and book store, and the depository of a circulating library. On the left two or three men are unloading wood, huge wagon-loads of which they have taken Sunday as a fit day for selling.

In the offering at church services several bags of gold dust came to me. In other parts of Idaho, as on all the Pacific coast, gold coin was the standard. And for several years I remember that greenbacks in Idaho passed at a settled rate of seventy-five cents to the dollar. Offerings at services in mining camps were seldom less than twenty-five dollars, and often were as much as seventy-five dollars.

On Sunday night I confirmed two women. Monday morning I visited a sick and dying miner named Hopkins. After prayer with him, I well remember his earnest thanks to me and his long holding of my hand and whispering "Sweet! Sweet!" referring to the prayers. In the afternoon I baptized two children. At night I met all interested in securing the services of a pastor. Twenty-four persons came and subscribed $1,400 per year on the spot.

Tuttle left Idaho by stagecoach and a week later arrived at his headquarters in Virginia City. He immediately went to the Planters' House for breakfast, then circulated in town to announce a church service in the evening at Tootle, Leach & Company's old deserted store. The room had been furnished with seats and nicknamed "Reception Hall." Tuttle commented, "As long as the novelty lasted of the new preacher and the Episcopal robes and the Prayer-Book services, large congregations came out, especially on Sunday evenings."

Finding meeting places was always a challenging task on his preaching tours. At one place they would meet in a saloon, while at another they might meet in a vacant cabin or store. Tuttle relates the story here of how he held meetings in a courthouse at one location:

We had service this morning in the courthouse. This courthouse was built as a church. The first preacher in it (Kingsley, a Methodist) dabbled in merchandise as well as preaching. While he was in the pulpit on Sunday, his clerks were selling goods from his store. After Kingsley retired, other preachers attempted to build up a congregation and complete and pay for the projected church. The last one here, a Methodist, paid from his own pocket the $1,500 debt resting on it. The people not supporting him, however, at his departure he sold it to the county for a courthouse in order to secure his money.

Based on these and other examples, Tuttle was determined to proceed cautiously with constructing Episcopal church buildings in Montana. His congregation was always very generous in their giving, and they were eager to provide financial support for pastors and teachers who ministered directly to them and their families. In this regard they were more interested in investing in people than in wood and stone. But the economy was in its infancy, and the population of the frontier towns was still very transient. Tuttle took his time and planned for the construction of buildings only where they were justified. Here he explains the steps that led to his first church in Virginia City:

> When I saw my way to build a church the people gathered to my help with abounding generosity. The way the building of the church came about was this. We had held our first services in the council chamber, the hall over a saloon, in which one branch of the Legislature had held its sittings. Then we moved to Reception Hall, which was the old deserted store of Tootle, Leach & Co. Then we occupied the deserted store of Erfort, Busch & Co. All the time I was thinking about a church building, but being determined not to move in any way that meant debt I did not see my way to move at all.

> Finally the Methodist minister, Rev. Mr. King, came among us, and with true Methodist enthusiasm and energy within a fortnight he set to work to build a church. I felt quite in the depths of meekness to see how in energy he was distancing me, yet for the life of me I could not see how I could wisely do other than I was doing. The frame of Mr. King's building went up, but before it was shingled and weather-boarded, and ere the minister had been three months in Virginia City, he left, shaking the dust of our town from his feet. He never appeared again and mechanics' liens were soon clapped upon the church.

> One of the Methodist trustees came to me of his own accord and told me of them. In conference with him I suggested that perhaps I might take hold and finish the church for one of our own. He replied: "It is just the thing for you to do. Here are fifty dollars remaining in my hands that I will turn over to you to help you in the matter." I therefore went to work to find out the amount of the liens. They were $1,286.74. I gave $500 myself and then prepared and passed a subscription book. I got such responses as justified me in pushing on, so I bought up the liens at about their face value, and when the sheriffs sale came I bought the property. I afterwards fin-

*First Episcopal Church in Virginia City, Montana.*

Courtesy of Special Collections, MSU Libraries, Bozeman, Montana, Collection 771.

ished the church at an entire cost of $3,409.08, and on the Sunday May 24, 1868, I entered it as "St. Paul's Church." The day we entered it I had the comfort of reporting to the congregation that every bill had been fully paid, and that there were sixteen dollars left over in the building account.

We had a most untoward time for moving yesterday in the rain and mud, yet we did move. I worked hard all day, carrying benches, picking up old lumber, shoveling away debris, etc. Yesterday when everything had been moved out of the old store and I was there alone, I kneeled down and tearfully thanked God for letting me preach for Him in those four walls, begging Him to forgive all I had said amiss, and praying that something I had spoken there might be as seed sown in good ground to spring up and bear fruit to His glory. My thoughts of the old store where I have labored and wept will ever be tender, even while glad and thankful thoughts spring up for the new church into which we have entered.

As his first winter in Montana began, Tuttle quite often found himself struggling with loneliness. To make his log cabin more homey, he got a white cat named "Dick."

I couldn't always keep free from fits of dreary lonesomeness, and Dick was then the greatest comfort to me. He would welcome me home from my walks, with all the joy a cat can show, and in the cabin would crawl up on my shoulder when I was reading or writing. At night his place was on the buffalo robe at the side or foot of my bed. Dear, faithful, friendly, old Dick! You were more of a help and

74

comfort to me that winter than ever your cat's brains could know, and to this day my heart warms to think of you!

Tuttle described that first winter by saying, "It was an anxious winter, it was a struggling winter, it was a lonely winter, but I never lost heart." He began to count his blessings. His health was excellent, and he thoroughly enjoyed the mountain climate with its dry, sunny, invigorating air. Each morning before breakfast he would read from the Bible, and after breakfast he would take long walks in the nearby mountains. He wrote, "These daily walks were to me a great delight. Eyes, lungs, legs, spirits, thoughts, were wonderfully refreshed and invigorated. A perfect reservoir of strength those steady long walks of the winter laid in for me." Tuttle would then return to his cabin to prepare his sermon for the week, and he said that those sermons written in a lonely cabin were "not the poorest in my barrel."

Reflecting on his first year in the mountains, Tuttle wrote:

> I find myself thinking of the year I spent in Virginia City as perhaps the most valuable one of my missionary experience. It furnished me ground for full sympathy with the clergy of the border. I was the immediate pastor of a frontier community, and could readily afterwards put myself in the place of any other pastor in considering his pastoral work. I knew the excitement of preaching to hundreds gathered. I knew the trial, when novelty and enthusiasm were gone, of preaching to ten and twelve. I realized in daily experience how hard and cold to spiritual things were the minds and thoughts of the men, and how hopeless it seemed to rouse or touch them by human effort. So it was easy for me to understand the confession of any downcast clergyman. "There is no one to be confirmed, there seems no spiritual growth," and not to make his sadness deeper by any harsh judgment on my part. It taught me loving forbearance towards wicked people. I did not compromise with their sin, I hope, but so good and kind were the people there to me personally, so true and loyal were they in their respect and helpfulness, that I could not help loving them, and my prayers for them were not perfunctory but heartfelt and warm. I wanted to be a friend to them, I tried to be a friend to them, I grew to be a friend to them, without, I hope, becoming in any way a partaker in their sins. I seemed to get a way of looking at wicked people, different from what I had before, and much more tender.

Many years later the Presbyterian church in Bozeman, Montana, celebrated its twenty-fifth anniversary, and Tuttle was invited to attend

75

the celebration. He commented, "In the letter of invitation occurred the following sentence: One of our members recently said, 'We always looked upon Bishop Tuttle as the people's bishop and felt that he was one of us.' This remark is suggestive of my relations to the whole field."

Daniel Tuttle would minister in the mountain communities of Montana, Idaho, and Utah until 1886. He traveled thousands of miles each year, and he was especially well-liked by the rough and rugged stagecoach drivers across the region. Tuttle not only planted churches, but he established schools and hospitals. He became a well-known and trusted preacher, advisor, and friend to the inhabitants of these Territories. As he was leaving his ministry in the mountains he wrote:

> I served as missionary bishop for nineteen years and four months. In my missionary field 3,809 have been baptized and 1,203 confirmed. In St. Mark's school and Rowland Hall, 3,186 boys and girls have been taught. In St. Mark's Hospital 4,776 patients have been cared for....These are the figures and facts. Who shall estimate the spiritual meaning and moral forces underlying and overlapping them? The mantle falls. The work is done. The change has come. The roll of stewardship for twenty years is closed up. God's mercy and forgiveness be upon it!

# The Presbyterian
# Dynamo

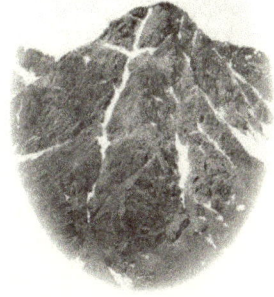

Early in 1870, Sheldon Jackson came to the Rocky Mountains for the first time. He rode the train to Cheyenne, Wyoming, which he described as "a city of shanties, only two years old, but of great prospective importance" on the railroad route. Jackson held a Sunday service in the schoolhouse, and that day he organized a church with only three members. He convinced the Union Pacific Railway Company to donate two town lots for a church building, and what would become a thriving congregation had its start. This was to be a typical day's work for Sheldon Jackson.

Born in 1834 near Schenectady, New York, Jackson graduated from Princeton Theological Seminary in 1855 and began his missionary career working among the Choctaw Indians. In the year that the transcontinental railroad was completed, Sheldon Jackson received an appointment from the Missouri River Presbytery as "Superintendent of Missions for Western Iowa, Nebraska, Dakota, Idaho, Montana, Wyoming, and Utah, or as Far as Our Jurisdiction Extends." By the summer of 1869, Jackson started a missionary tour of the West, making use of railroad and stagecoach lines to carry him quickly from place to place.

Contemporaries called Sheldon Jackson either a visionary or a rebel. Previously, the Presbyte-

*Sheldon Jackson,*
*Presbyterian Minister*

rian mission policy involved waiting until a community was well established before engaging in any church-planting efforts. One of his protégés later commented:

> I do not think it is too much to say that Sheldon Jackson's entrance upon this work marked a radical change in the spirit and methods of conducting home mission work and was a great step forward... Those who had the shaping of our policy in their hands seemed to be perpetually haunted with the fear of boom towns and the spectre of dead churches. And so rather than organize one church that might soon prove a failure, they would miss the starting of a dozen that would have lived and prospered...Sheldon Jackson, with the spirit of the true pioneer, at once adopted a bolder and more aggressive policy. The missionary was sent and the church established with the advent of the first immigrants, and these became magnets and centers toward which Christian institutions and activities crystallized... Under his leadership the Presbyterian Church assumed its full share of responsibility for the evangelization of the great West, and whatever had been its failure in the past, now stood in the very front rank of those who were fighting to win the land for Christ.

Following the main transportation routes, Jackson continued his missionary tour westward over South Pass to the Sweetwater mining region. Leaving the railroad, Jackson boarded the stagecoach and was furnished with a loaded rifle to defend himself against Indian attacks along the route. The mule team raced at full speed from station to station, and fortunately there was no attack. They reached South Pass City in safety, and there Jackson was led to an "untidy room, twelve feet square, in which were three double beds. The basin of a mountain stream in back of the hotel furnished the only available place for morning ablutions. The charge for accommodations of this character was four dollars per day."

Jackson posted a notice announcing preaching services, and an hour later a boy was sent out with a bell to say, "There will be preaching this evening!" That service was held in a large warehouse. The next day he departed on the stage for Helena, Montana, which was a journey of five hundred miles taking four days. Arriving on a Saturday, Jackson visited more than a hundred homes and businesses to record the names of those interested in starting a Presbyterian church. These personal calls were very effective, and the next day Jackson held two services, after which he organized a church with twelve members. At the time, this was the only Presbyterian church within a thousand miles.

Everywhere Jackson stopped he would hold services, select town lots for church buildings, and rally the community to support a new Presbyterian congregation. At one place the mosquitoes almost foiled the attempt to start a new church. The meeting was held in a schoolhouse, and before the appointed time a man used a smoking smudge pot to clear the room. Despite the smoke, the mosquitoes gathered in such a swarm that "it was not deemed expedient to preach." People remained long enough, however, to record their interest, elect elders, and officially organize the congregation—after which everyone hastily retreated from the hostile attackers.

During his first missionary tour, Jackson traveled 2,300 miles by railroad and 1,200 miles by stagecoach. At every stopping place, and regardless of his physical condition, he energetically pushed ahead with his work. The record shows that within a single month Jackson had organized eight new Presbyterian churches in three Territories. Jackson immediately returned East to secure funding for church buildings and pastoral salaries. He was very effective as a fund-raiser and promoter, even securing free passes for railroad and stagecoach travel from the major companies.

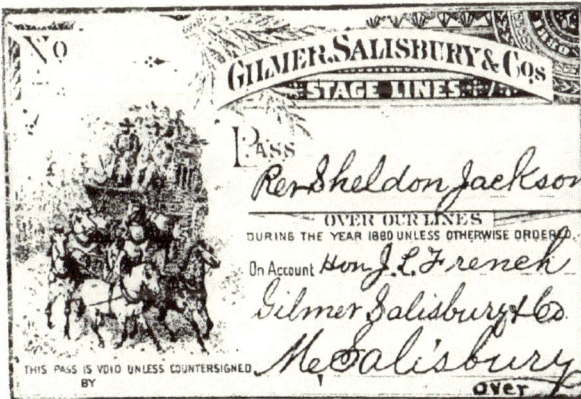

*Free pass for stagecoach travel, issued to Sheldon Jackson.*
Reprinted from Stewart (1908), 134.

Jackson also received permission from the governing board to organize the new Presbytery of Colorado, which included the Territories of Colorado, Wyoming, Utah, Montana, and northern New Mexico. He immediately made travel arrangements to convene the new regional organization at Denver. The railroad would not reach Denver until June 1870, so Jackson rode all night on the stagecoach from Cheyenne to arrive in Denver on February 18th. He jumped down from the stage-coach, arranged to use the basement of the Baptist church, and officially convened the Presbytery by preaching the opening sermon. Half of the churches enrolled in the Presbytery had been started by Jackson on his latest missionary tour.

Almost immediately Jackson booked passage on the south-bound stagecoach over the "Stormy Divide," known today as the Palmer Divide which separates the watersheds of the Platte and Arkansas Rivers. He traveled in that coach with a rancher, a former legislator, a Spanish speculator, a French miner, and an invalid from the East. Here he describes the conditions and events of his trip:

> All were heavily armed, and the principal topic of conversation was a horse race which was to take place in the southern part of the territory the next day. The fumes of tobacco smoke became so dense that the missionary was obliged to take refuge with the driver on the box outside. His destination was reached in safety late in the night. The next morning diligent search was made for members of the Presbyterian Church, but without success. As he went from house to house that morning, he was met with the response, "There are none in this section." While making an attempt to secure a building belonging to the Methodist Church for a public meeting, a man came up to him in haste, as if fearful he might escape him, and said: "I am John Irvine, a Presbyterian elder. I have heard that you are a Presbyterian minister, and I want you to come with me to my home."
>
> "Yes, I am," was the reply, "And I will go with you with pleasure. Where do you live?" "About twenty-five miles down there," said the man, pointing in the direction he expected to take. This reply was a little startling, but Jackson affirmed his acceptance. A good pair of mules made the miles appear short, and in due time the ranch of John Irvine was reached. The next morning Irvine's son was mounted on a bronco and sent to summon the people of the neighborhood to a preaching service that evening. At the appointed time an attentive congregation numbering sixty persons was assembled in two of the adjacent rooms of the house.

Jackson spent two days there, and on the morning of the third day he was given a horse to ride to the city of Pueblo, Colorado, on the Arkansas River. The following Sunday he preached to a large group which gathered at the courthouse, filling the place to overflowing. He organized the first Presbyterian church in Pueblo that day, with John Irvine as the ruling elder. Jackson wrote, "The preciousness of such scenes as were witnessed on that Sabbath in this frontier village, must be seen and felt to be realized. Could our young ministers know of the joy of such labors, they would the more earnestly ask to be sent to the front."

Jackson turned north again, and the following day he organized a Presbyterian church at Colorado City with five members. After returning to Denver, Jackson immediately left for Georgetown, Black Hawk, Idaho Springs, and Golden where he organized churches. Within two weeks, Jackson had traveled five hundred miles and organized six churches. He next started a church at Greeley, Colorado, which had been settled by the Union Colony, a utopian temperance community organized by a group of New Yorkers. In the adjacent settlement of Evans, Colorado, another church was established as well.

In many places where the transient population made it difficult to plant permanent congregations, Jackson would preach and minister as he had the opportunity during his travels. One of Jackson's contemporaries noted the following example from his tours in Colorado:

> At a mining camp on Mount Bross, where as yet only two of the workmen had brought their families and were living in homes, the question was asked, "Do you ever have preaching up here?"
>
> "Oh yes," was the reply, "Sheldon Jackson was here last Sunday and we all met in that building, a house for crushing ore, the largest in the place. He stood on the engine and gave us a rousing sermon." That is the sort of men needed in these frontier settlements—men who can stand on an engine and preach. My friend Jackson would not hesitate, if he thought he could reach an old hardened sinner, to mount a locomotive and let fly a Gospel message at a group by the wayside while going at a speed of forty miles an hour.

One winter Jackson was delayed on his circuit for three days because of heavy snow and drifts along the Stormy Divide between Denver and Colorado City. On another occasion he was waiting on a lonely road to board a stagecoach for Pueblo, Colorado, and was mistaken for an outlaw:

> It so happened that the coach, which was due at this point about midnight, carried on that trip a sheriff and his posse who were bringing a noted desperado to the county seat for trial. While on the way this party had received notice that an attempt would be made at some point to hold up the stagecoach and rescue the prisoner. When

Jackson appeared by the roadside between stations at this unseemly hour and signaled the driver to stop, the guards naturally associated him with the leadership of a band of brigands in ambush. Before he could explain the situation, a half dozen revolvers, thrust out from the coach, covered his person at close range and the ominous click of the hammers warned him that there was but the trembling of a finger between him and instant death. It is needless to say that he surrendered unconditionally, and when the whole matter was made clear was cordially welcomed into the coach.

About this time Jackson began publishing the *Rocky Mountain Presbyterian* newspaper, "with the design of bringing the Presbyterians of the territories into closer communication with each other, and also of making the churches of the East acquainted with the urgent needs and marvelous possibilities of this new land." This little publication was one of the few religious newspapers in Colorado at the time, and it was sent free of charge to anyone who wanted to receive it. One man commented, "This writer has seen scores of letters of appreciation for the helpful information received through its columns, and in one of these there is mention of a gift of $500 which was sent to assist in the expense of its publication. Thus with pen and tongue and pictorial illustration the living realities of the mission work on the frontier were kept before the minds of the Church and its ministry." This publication was able to travel to many out-of-the-way corners of the Rocky Mountains that would have otherwise been inaccessible to the missionaries.

Jackson also made several trips into New Mexico. At that time the Denver & Rio Grande Railroad had reached Pueblo, Colorado, from which point Jackson made the rest of the journey by stagecoach. There had been heavy thunderstorms in southern Colorado, which caused flash flooding and delays for travelers. At one point they received word

Sheldon Jackson, Editor.    Denver, Colorado, March, 1872.    Vol 1  No 1

Reprinted from Stewart (1908), 322.

that the road over Raton Pass had washed out. While waiting at a stage station, Jackson was able to get breakfast at one o'clock in the morning, after which he wrapped himself in his overcoat and slept soundly on a billiard table until the stagecoach resumed its journey several hours later. Their road led southward through Las Vegas, Santa Fe, Albuquerque, and Silver City. Along this route Jackson would "attempt to sleep under difficulties. A sudden lurch would jam my head against the coach, or a jolt toss me up, to come down with a thud."

Another night he was awakened by a crash, followed by a volley of oaths. In the darkness his coach had run into another coach coming up the ravine. The lamps were smashed and the wheels and whiffletrees were securely locked together. In the dark, they were finally able to separate the coaches and resume their journey. Here Jackson describes another of his trips on which a buckboard wagon was substituted for the regular stagecoach:

> There were four hundred pounds of mail heaped in front and back, so there was no alternative but to sit bolt upright. Once I started to crouch down between the seat and dashboard, but, small as I am, it could not be done with comfort. So strapping myself to the seat lest I should get to sleep and fall off, I got through the night as best I could. There were no houses between stations. The first stop west of Silver City was thirty-five miles, which we made in five hours. There we took supper of two fried eggs, fried beef, and a cup of coffee. The charge for this wayside meal was one dollar. There was a cañon at this place which showed up distinctly in the light of the full moon. Our next station was twenty-two miles distant. We had a pair of wild horses and made the distance in three hours. At this station there were four men who were evidently equipped for instant attack or defense. Their house was an armory of guns and revolvers.

After this harrowing trip, Jackson refreshed himself with a cup of tea and immediately met with six local residents to organize yet another Presbyterian church.

On his third visit to New Mexico he was accompanied by Alexander M. Darley, whom Jackson had commissioned as a minister in the San Luis Valley of southern Colorado. It was fortunate that they were traveling in a light buckboard wagon pulled by only two horses.

> A few miles out from Fort Garland there was a severe storm of hail, snow, and sleet, in which we rode three or four hours without cover

or umbrella. Made Conejos the first day and put up at a Mexican house where we had coffee without milk, stewed mutton, and tortillas for supper, and the same for breakfast. Ten miles west of Conejos, we commenced climbing the mountains, and from thence on it was up and up, the snow increasing from one inch to a foot in depth. The new military road exists only in imagination as yet. It has been staked out and blazed through the woods, but not graded, and some tracks had been made by pilgrims like ourselves, supposing there really was a road there. The first teams were thirty days in getting over sixty miles and a number were two weeks on the way. We made it in two days, but at great risk to life and limb.

About one PM on Thursday, we trotted over the edge of a precipitous slope of about 1,000 feet, not seeing it until we made the turn of the descent. I sprang out. Darley instantly put on the brakes, but they would not hold, and soon the broncos were on a full run. The wagon flew through the air as it bounded from rock to rock and our blankets and provisions strewed the road. I gave up the team for lost, when one of the broncos concluded to balk. The momentum was so great, however, that he slid along about fifty feet before the wagon came to a stop, and not a step farther would he budge. We finally took the team off, and chaining both wheels, let the wagon down the mountain by hand.

From this point we toiled through cañons, bogs, over fallen timber and rocks, until night overtook us on the summit, at an elevation of 10,000 feet. We drove into a thick clump of tall pines and camped. The snow was nearly two feet deep, and the cold was intense. I judge below zero. With great labor we heaped up a pile of logs three or four feet high for a fire, which sent the sparks to the top of the tallest pines and lighted up the woods all around. The horses were tied on one side of the fire to protect them from the mountain lions, and we laid pine boughs on top of the snow for our bed. We took turns at sleeping and watching during the night.

Next morning, we were on the way about sunrise, and during the forenoon were able to make only one mile an hour. Twice we had to take the team off, lock the wheels, turn the wagon around, and let it down a mountainside backward with ropes by hand from one to two thousand feet. At one point, Mr. Darley gave up completely and declared we might as well abandon the wagon at last. But I told him we could try, and if we got down safely, all right, and if the thing went to the bottom with a smash, it was not much worse than to abandon it at the top. After a severe struggle, however, we did get down safely at about 2 PM.

We passed out of the mountains into the valley. The rest of the afternoon we made from six to eight miles an hour, and reached the Indian agency after nightfall. Have made arrangements to preach at the Chicago colony, six miles above, tomorrow. There are eight families in this settlement. Mr. Darley and agent Russell are now visiting some of the Mexican plazas. The smallpox is raging all through this region, and is proving very fatal. Taos, the objective point of this journey, was reached on the fourth day out.

When he returned to the meeting of the Colorado Presbytery after his journey through New Mexico, one newspaper reporter marveled: "It is hard to keep track of this brother. It is worth a man's life almost to keep in sight even of his coat-tail, as he glides around the mountains or plunges into deep ravines, or darts away southward among a strange and wild people. On this trip he had travelled 3,000 miles."

One newspaper writer described Sheldon Jackson as "a small, compact, well-knit, sinewy, sanguine, sunburnt young man. We are surprised to find in such a form the great religious explorer and founder of churches all over the western section of the United States." Another of Jackson's contemporaries gave the following description: "In my judgment the chief elements in his career of phenomenal success were indomitable energy, utter disregard of obstacles or difficulties, absolute fearlessness along the line of what he saw to be duty."

Jackson seemed to have the energy of ten men. He kept up a constant ministry circuit, while at the same time writing for the newspaper, dealing with the administrative tasks of the Presbytery, and raising funds for the work on the frontier. One companion commented:

We have known him to travel for forty-eight hours in a stage coach, reaching his destination in the morning, preaching three times on the day of his arrival, arranging for the salary of a pastor, and laying the foundations of a temporary manse, which was completed and occupied by a young minister and his wife before the next Sabbath. And a few days later, perhaps, in Utah or Montana, printed placards announce that this untiring evangelist will preach in the hall above a lager beer saloon, or in the dining-room of a hotel.

Another contemporary described him similarly:

I have known him to preach three times in one day, riding twenty-five miles on horseback between appointments, and rise the next morning fresh and ready for anything. One evening he preached in Missoula and at the close of the service he took the stage for a hundred miles, over a mountain road—a steady twenty-four hour run—to Deer Lodge, where he arrived barely in time for a service which he had announced for that evening. He persuaded the driver to take him directly to the church, and leaping from the top of the coach to the church steps, entered it and went through the service without a moment for rest or refreshment of any kind.

The statement made by someone as illustrating his habits of industry, that he edited the *Rocky Mountain Presbyterian* from the deck of stagecoaches, was hardly an exaggeration. I have seen Dr. Jackson sway vast assemblies, and I have seen him where two or three were gathered together in humble cabins or dugouts. I have seen him in some of the high places of the earth, and I have seen him sleeping on the ground among the sage brush and in stables among the cattle, and everywhere and always he is the same imperturbable, irrepressible, unpretentious Sheldon Jackson.

During his years of Rocky Mountain ministry, Jackson covered almost 350,000 miles, an average of about 27,000 miles each year. He traveled by train, stagecoach, wagon, horseback, and on foot to reach as many people on the frontier as he could. Jackson braved the entire gamut of discomforts and hardships, from miserable roads and trails, to the threat of wild beasts and hostile men. Three times the newspapers prematurely reported his death, and one Chicago paper erred by actually printing his obituary. He established dozens of churches and schools in places where the Presbyterian Church had feared to tread only a few years before his arrival. The results of this great man's ministry are evident across the West to this day.

# Still More Ground to Cover

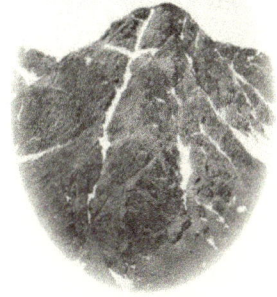

G old and other resources for exploitation were constantly being discovered in the "New West" at the end of the nineteenth century. Each fresh discovery opened new areas for settlement and provided new opportunities for itinerant preachers. Early in the 1870s the Home Missionary Society commissioned J.D. Kingsbury for an extended tour of Idaho Territory. He reported the following experiences:

> I went into the saloons and said to the men, "I am to preach in the Opera House." They replied, "That's right, elder, we need it." Blotched, filthy, delirious, yet sobered at once by the very thought of religion to which early years were no stranger, they said: "Give us your hand, elder, we fellers need it." We secured a hall, the people came gladly, the hall was filled. The Spirit of God was in the place, and hearts were touched. A church was formed. Interest was deep and tender. The little mining city had a new atmosphere. It was a transformation. We had hoped and prayed and labored, expecting great things, but the results were so much greater than we were looking for that we forgot our own feeble service and said reverently in our hearts: "Behold what God hath wrought."

An insightful piece appeared in the *Rocky Mountain Directory and Colorado Gazetteer* for 1871. It specifically addressed the connection between "gold fever" and the tendency to neglect spiritual development. This article, however, shows that religion was not shunted aside by the early pioneers and explorers entering Colorado Territory in search of gold and other economic opportunities.

> No avocation so completely engrosses every sentiment of the human heart as the search for gold. As this was the leading pursuit of the earlier settlers of Colorado, it would not have been strange if religious interests had been neglected, but such was not the case, and it speaks well for the hardy pioneers when it can be said that many of them were and still remain in the front ranks of religious progress, and that they have been the bearers of Christianity and civilization wherever the attractions of glittering gold allure them...The Presbyterians, Congregationalists, and Baptists have churches and church organizations in all the principle cities and towns in the Territory... There are few settlements of any importance that are not included in the circuit system of the Methodist church.

Men pushed farther and higher into the Rocky Mountains, and everywhere they went they were followed by the intrepid home missionaries. Even in the remotest locations, itinerant preachers were welcomed by the rugged settlers. Here Methodist preacher John Dyer describes his experience reaching the high-altitude mines along the Mosquito Range in Colorado:

> I had a famous climb up Mt. Lincoln. Mine after mine had been opened in that region. The Dolly Varden was working with quite a force, the Moose with scores of miners, the Russia with twenty, and at the base of the mountain was Dudley, a village with a furnace. A number of preachers had passed that way, but apparently the thought of preaching to the cliff-dwellers never entered their minds. It was, indeed, an achievement to ascend Mt. Lincoln, one of the highest Rocky Mountain peaks. I concluded that I would go up and preach. On Tuesday I started on foot five miles to the first mine. Just as I got above timber, the wind met me with a heavy squall of snow, and although it was some time till night, the air was soon so thick with snow that I could not see from one telegraph pole to another. I wished the wire had been put six feet from the ground, then I could have held to it. As it was, I felt along the wagon ruts, and could go only a few feet at a time without bracing myself on my pole and resting for breath.

> It was almost impossible to make headway against the wind and snow coming down the mountain. The road went close to the dump of the Dolly Varden mine and the shaft house and boarding house. It

was so dark I could not see even the dump, but as I turned my face back to rest I had got past the house and above the dump. I thought the house must be close. I saw the sparks come out of the chimney, and was only three rods from it. My face was dripping with thawing snow, and my strength nearly exhausted. I was let into Mr. Hall's room, the superintendent of the mine. He seemed surprised that I had got through, although he had given out the appointment for me. He made me welcome, and as I started into the dining room he surprised me by putting a five dollar bill into my hand. I tried to preach to eleven hearers. Ten of that number each laid down a dollar on the table without being asked.

The next day I called at the Moose mine, where there were sixty men. I told the cook I was on a preaching excursion, and would be there the next night to talk to them. He said he would tell the men. I went on to Australia, the highest mine worked, within three hundred feet of the top of Mt. Lincoln, where I found twenty men. I had a good visit with the superintendent and preached to them. They were very attentive and respectful, but forgot to carry around the hat. On my way back I preached to about forty-five, had good attention, and when the benediction was pronounced one of the number passed a hat and took up sixteen dollars. This was the first preaching on Mt. Lincoln. I was back several times, but otherwise services have been few. I want to say here that in all my experience I do not remember an instance where a miner or prospector came to my preaching who did not behave himself.

Episcopal minister Daniel Tuttle could echo Dyer's conclusion based on his experiences on the gold frontier in Montana. Sunday seemed to be the only day when men could come to the settlements for supplies or amusement, but they were usually respectful of a preacher's efforts. Here Tuttle explained this, as well as describing a time when his singing literally shook the meeting place:

In Bannack scarcely any other religious services are ever held than my yearly ones. The Sunday I was there, the inhabitants thoughtfully suspended for once their customary weekly sports of horse running, foot-racing, and cock-fighting, and came to the services. In the evening the floor gave way in the upper room while we were singing the hymn before sermon. It sank four inches. We all expected it to go utterly down. I am a great admirer of bravery, coolness, presence of mind, unselfishness, and I have commended these virtues. But the humiliating fact to be told is that when the floor gave forth that awful cracking, I was the first to spring out of the door nearby, at the back, and down the stairs, in wildly-streaming robes. When my own feet were on terra firma I was full of valuable courage and forethought, and I shouted to the surging congregation: "Don't rush, don't push, you'll break the stairs, you'll crush the children." That kind of courage provokes a smile, doesn't it? A carpenter went below and examined the building. An important under-prop had given way. We could come back and be safe, he said, if we would remain near the sides of the building leaving the center unburdened. So, a little ashamed of myself, I went back. Many of the people, also, though not all, came back, and we finished our usual services and sermon. It was of God's merciful goodness that the floor of that huge building, whose roof and sides were logs, did not go down and crush us to death.

In the late 1870s there were new silver strikes which revived what had been Oro City in California Gulch, and the boom town of Leadville, Colorado, was born. During its rough and tumble history, Leadville gained a reputation for being the "wickedest city on earth." One of the first missionary preachers to stake his claim on Leadville was Methodist Thomas Uzzell. The story was told that "Parson Tom" buried over three hundred people during his ministry in Leadville, almost none of whom died from natural causes.

Like so many successful frontier preachers, Uzzell had a simple, sincere, friendly style which endeared him to the people. A contemporary newspaper account reported, "In those days he was frequently placed in positions in which any other man's life would have been endangered, but somehow Parson Tom's honest simplicity always stood him in good stead, and he made friends instead of enemies even among outlaws. The wickedest men in camp respected him, and they gave liberally to his church. Although he never succeeded in turning many of them from evil, they invariably came to him when in trouble."

Methodist Minister, Thomas A. Uzzell

The people of Leadville always sent for Parson Tom when they felt death approaching. One day Uzzell was summoned to a house of ill repute to pray with one of the young girls who had been shot by a drunken cowboy. They thought the girl would soon die, and Parson Tom shared the gospel of salvation through Jesus Christ. As it turned

*Men on the porch of a storefront church on the main street of Leadville, Colorado.*
Courtesy of History Colorado, William Henry Jackson Collection: 20004631

out the girl named Kate did not die, but professed her faith in God and went on to become an honest woman and a faithful wife.

Uzzell himself said, "The town was hell bent, and in most cases I think it gained its objective...They died hard, but they always wanted me with 'em." Here Parson Tom shares his experience during one of the many funerals at which he officiated in Leadville:

> It was strange that I didn't get hurt in that town. I used to go at all hours of the day and night, answering death-bed calls and visiting the sick, but never a word was ever said against me or my work. One full experience was at a funeral. Cole and Alexander ran the worst dance hall there—a perfect den of vice. From five hundred to fifteen-hundred men would gather in the big building every night, drink, carouse, shoot lights out, and dance with the tough women. Jim Cole is now a respectable ranch man not far from Denver, and always a big-hearted fellow. He often told me he would come to my Sunday school, only every fellow in town would make fun of him.
>
> Alexander died and Jim wanted me to preach a funeral over him. Well, I did and those fellows got the truth right from the shoulder. Every gambler, saloon man, and bad woman in town turned out, as they always did upon such occasions, and I told them about the separation of sheep from the goats on that last day of all. Many of them winced, but there was no trouble.

91

The cemetery was four or five miles out, and there was snow on the ground. You never saw such a cortege as that. Wagons, buckboards, sleighs, burros, broncos, everything went. I rode out with a man, and after the service at the grave people passed by to take a last look at the face of their dead friend. When Jim came by he said: "Well, Parson, you gave us hell, but I guess we all deserved it. Here's a fifty dollar note."

The man who brought me out forgot me and went back alone, and before I realized it every vehicle there other than an express wagon had gone. Three boards had been placed across the wagon body for seats, and six notorious women occupied them. Discovering my predicament they called to me, and said it was a shame to bring a parson out there and leave him to walk home in the snow, and invited me to ride with them. I wasn't married then, and the thought flashed through my mind, "What will the good Leadville people say when they see their parson riding with such women?" But it was either that or walk, and I didn't walk. The women made me sit between two of them on the middle seat, and so I was surrounded by them. When we reached the edge of town I told them I had some business to attend to and would get out and walk the rest of the way. I think they must have suspected my scheme, for they insisted on carrying me to the very door of the parsonage, right through the two busiest streets of the town. Well, that made a big sensation; the people never stopped teasing me about it, and the newspaper made the most of it.

Meanwhile, in Montana Territory, there were fresh gold discoveries and another young preacher was answering the call. William Wesley Van Orsdel would become known affectionately throughout Montana as "Brother Van." He grew up in a Christian home in Pennsylvania and was granted an exhorter's license in the Methodist Episcopal Church at the age of seventeen. In 1870 he began working his way west, first as a day laborer in an oil field, which gave him enough money to reach Chicago. There he met Chaplain McCabe, secretary of the Board of Church Extension. After listening to Brother Van preach, McCabe said, "You are on the right track, young man. Go west to Montana and help to build the kingdom in the western wilds."

Traveling to Sioux City, Iowa, Brother Van began assisting a local missionary preacher by establishing Sunday Schools, singing, and preaching. As soon as a boat was ready to steam up the Missouri River, Brother Van negotiated passage to Fort Benton in Montana Territory.

The fare was $100, but Brother Van did not have that much money. The captain asked him why he was going to Montana, and the young missionary replied, "To sing and pray, and to encourage people to be good." That phrase was to become Brother Van's motto for the rest of his ministry in the West, and it convinced the captain to give him passage, "if you will sing and preach for us."

Arriving in Fort Benton on a Sunday, Brother Van immediately set about to gather a group in the saloon for preaching. Steamboat officers, freighters, cowboys, Indians, and set-

*Brother Van on horseback.*
Reprinted from Brummitt (1919), frontispiece.

tlers attended his first sermon in Montana. When he noticed their attention drifting, he would launch into one of the old familiar hymns that some of them remembered from back East. He was eagerly invited to preach in the evening to an even larger congregation. A woman who attended that service opened her home to him and was the first person to establish what would become a tradition throughout Montana, "Brother Van's Room."

Within a week Van Orsdel pushed west toward Fort Shaw, riding in an army wagon across the prairie. It had rained heavily and the road was extremely muddy. The army mules balked and refused to pull, so the driver "spoke to the errant beasts." He then remembered that there was a preacher in the wagon, and he apologized for his language. Brother Van laughed and replied, "Why, bless your soul, you express my sentiments exactly, though I can't approve of your language."

After gathering a group of soldiers in the garrison, Brother Van won their respect with his sincere, friendly personality and his obvious concern for their welfare. The next day he left the safety of the fort to visit the Blackfoot Indian agency near the base of the mountains. During his first meeting with the Indians, they began to catch the spirit of brotherhood in his words and manner. Eventually Brother Van would become a close friend of the tribe, whose members gave him the name "Great Heart."

Brother Van then set out for the gold camps near Helena, Montana. He preached there as well as in Bozeman, Butte, Bannack, Virginia City, and all parts in between. He began riding his horse along this circuit, and even extended his reach into Idaho. In one remote location a miner commented, "If a herd of wild buffalo had run through the streets of St. Louis it could not have caused more comment than that a preacher had come to town." By the end of his first year he had organized seven new churches with one hundred fifty new members. Everywhere he went, Brother Van won the hearts and the friendship of the people.

In 1877 the previously peaceful Nez Perce Indians began raiding and killing settlers across the region. US Army General Oliver O. Howard, known as the "Christian General," was sent to quell these uprisings. Because of his knowledge of both the country and the Indians, Brother Van was enlisted as a scout and adviser. In addition, he continued his work of preaching, singing, and encouraging the terrified people of the area.

While Brother Van was preaching to a large group of people at the courthouse in the town of Bannack, guards were posted to watch for an Indian attack. The people were upset and the preacher quieted their fears with this sermon text:

> He that dwelleth in the secret place of the Most High shall abide under the shadow of the Almighty. I will say of the Lord, He is my refuge and my fortress: my God; in him will I trust. Surely he shall deliver thee from the snare of the fowler, and from the noisome pestilence. He shall cover thee with his feathers, and under his wings shalt thou trust: his truth shall be thy shield and buckler. Thou shalt not be afraid for the terror by night; nor for the arrow that flieth by day; Nor for the pestilence that walketh in darkness; nor for the destruction that wasteth at noonday. A thousand shall fall at thy side, and ten thousand at thy right hand; but it shall not come nigh thee. (Psalm 91:1-7)

At dawn a rider arrived in Bannack to warn of an imminent attack, and Van Orsdel was one of two scouts sent to report on the raiders' position. By crawling and making use of available cover, they evaded the Indian war party, located a missing man, and found the bodies of four victims. The dead men were taken to Bannack for burial, and Brother Van officiated at the service.

That funeral is a sacred hour in Montana history. The terrified people gathered in a great sobbing congregation. The isolation of the settlers gave them a feeling of desolation that was disheartening. The services began and the preacher in his own quieting way talked to the living, for hope was his vital breath. Comfort began to steal over the waiting throng, when a messenger appeared at the church door. He said, "The Indians are again approaching Bannack." The service came to an abrupt close. They decided that word of the new attack must be taken to General Howard, who was coming toward the scene and was even then but twelve miles away. Once more Brother Van offered his services and with John Poindexter set out for help.

On hearing of the danger that threatened Bannack, General Howard dispatched a company of cavalry for the town's protection. He then spoke to the two seasoned scouts who had come to him for help, and he explained the importance of sending information to Washington concerning the serious situation, asking them if they would be his messengers to the nearest point of communication with the government. So in the lonely watches of the night, John Poindexter and Brother Van started on another errand of mercy. As they left the camp they could hear the hoot of the owl and the yelp of the coyote—sounds that to these two scouts were full of deadly meaning. They knew that the hoot and the yelp were signals given by watching Indians.

As silently as possible they moved, going directly to the south, and as they journeyed the calls grew indistinct, and at last were heard no more. The scouts relaxed slightly, but suddenly in the dim dawn twelve warriors loomed up before them. No shots could be fired. The party was small and a shot would call other waiting Indians to their assistance. General Howard must not be drawn into needless battle, for his men and horses were suffering for lack of rest. The horses which the scouts were riding were fresh and spirited, so, giving spur and riding in furious haste, the two messengers outdistanced the Indians, leaving them and the immediate danger far behind.

At last the scouts reached the stage road, and rode without interruption to a station. Here the precious message to Washington was put in the hands of the stagecoach drivers who carried passengers and letters across the Great American Desert. Their duty accomplished, Brother Van and his companion returned to the seat of war. They found Bannack ready for a siege. The town was full of people and their need of solace was great. A church building had been started

*Methodist Church dedicated by Brother Van in Bannack, Montana,*
*shortly after the Indian uprising which threatened the town.*
Courtesy of Library of Congress Prints and Photographs Division.

but the Indian wars had halted the work. The missionary scout determined to finish the church and he found that everybody wanted to help. Soldiers, settlers, and cowboys went at the building with hearty good will. The little church was thus very speedily completed.

What the helpful presence of the preacher-scout meant to the distressed townspeople in those trying days is shown by a dispatch sent from Bannack to the *Helena Herald*, August, 1877. The correspondent reported: "The Rev. Van Orsdel is here doing duty as a volunteer. He is a whole man. God bless all good men of whatever creed."

After the Indian uprising, Brother Van continued his preaching circuit. His singing voice helped him call the people to services, and he would stand outdoors on a hillside to start a rousing chorus of "Shall We Gather at the River." The miners, gamblers, shopkeepers, and settlers were irresistibly drawn to him. One gambler said, "I like that old scout; he plays fair." Everyone liked his simple, sweet message and his friendly style.

The song "The Gospel Train is Coming" particularly pleased them, for the railroad language held new and fascinating words in a community just growing accustomed to the railroad. One of the men said to the preacher, "If you will sing that song tomorrow night, I'll bring forty men to hear you." "All right, that's a bargain," said the singer. This man was the leader of a gang, and he had a hurdy-gurdy which made his saloon especially attractive. On the next night forty grizzled men marched in and took their seats. No disturbance was made by the forty who had reserved seats, but something else did happen: that hurdy-gurdy man got on board the "Gospel Train" and brought along a number of his comrades.

On one occasion a local preacher planned to take a collection for Brother Van's salary, and in the morning service the collection fell short. However, in the afternoon service one man put all the required funds in the hat for Brother Van. One of his friends later told the preacher the story of those funds.

> Two men at the service on Sunday morning remembered afterward that Brother Van's salary was short, and they agreed to play cards for the money in the afternoon collection. If A. won, the money was to go to Brother Van; if B. did, Brother Van lost. Word went around and the saloon filled with people to watch the game. If A. won, the crowd would yell, "The Lord gets that!" and if B. was lucky, "That goes to the devil!" In the end, A. won and Brother Van's salary was paid by the successful gambler. Upon hearing this story, the preacher said, "I'm so glad we got that money. It has been in the hands of the devil long enough. Brother Van will put it to a better use."

As the region began to grow, Van Orsdel became concerned for the education of the children and decided that Montana should have a Christian college. Over the course of a decade he founded and nurtured a struggling school in Helena, Montana, which eventually became Montana Wesleyan University.

Brother Van often ministered to sick and dying miners, cowboys, and settlers, but as the years passed he determined that Montana should have a modern medical facility. After years of planning and prayer, he and his people opened a new Christian hospital with all of the latest conveniences. It was named the "Deaconess Hospital," later called the Montana Deaconess Medical Center (now part of the Benefis Health System). Brother Van had always opposed gambling and drunkenness. He hated that business, but he loved and befriended the men involved in it, and they knew the difference. Those men decided to do something for Brother Van, and they began putting away money for him. When Brother Van eventually found out about the money, he immediately used it to build a nurses home and training school across the street from the new hospital.

During the years of his ministry in Montana, Van Orsdel built one hundred churches, six hospitals, and two colleges. He had stepped off the steamboat at Fort Benton in a rugged wilderness, and after almost fifty years of ministry he had helped to build a modern State. Brother Van died on December 19, 1919, and was buried in Helena, Montana. Every year he always sent out a large number of Christmas cards, and he had arranged for his 1919 Christmas cards to be sent with the message "My first Christmas in Heaven."

# Adventures on Colorado's Western Slope

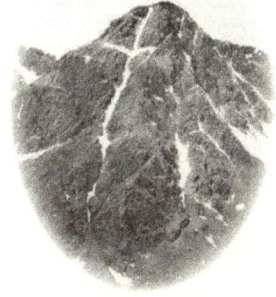

The mountains along the western portion of the Continental Divide in southwestern Colorado are very steep, rugged, and remote. Yet this inhospitable area proved to be one of the most highly mineralized regions in the Colorado Rockies. By the mid-1870s, rich gold and silver deposits were being discovered in the San Juan Mountains. This sparked a new mining boom around the Lake City area, and the typical cycle of settlement began to take place. Prospectors in tents and log cabins attracted suppliers who built cabins and shacks. These were soon followed by more permanent settlements of frame buildings using sawn lumber, and eventually structures of stone and brick.

From a spiritual perspective, the San Luis Valley in south-central Colorado had already been "prospected" by both the Methodists and the Presbyterians. Sheldon Jackson had enlisted the aid of Alexander M. Darley to cover this region. But it was a vast area, and in the short time since his arrival Alexander Darley had not been able to explore beyond the Continental Divide to the west.

In the spring of 1875 the Rev. Alexander M. Darley was sent to Del Norte with instructions to itinerate in all the accessible regions round about, and, if the way should be clear, to make a visit to the San Juan country, on the western slope of the Sierra Madre range, into which multitudes were going to search for gold. By previous appointment, the superintendent met Mr. Darley at Del Norte and assisted him in the organization of a church at that place on the 11th of April. Mr. Darley had the privilege of preaching the first Presbyterian sermon in that portion of the state which lies to the west of the Sangre de Christo Mountains.

Alexander had a younger brother, George M. Darley, who left a lucrative career as a mechanic to study for the ministry. In 1876 George Darley traveled by train to La Veta, Colorado, in the foothills east of the Sangre de Cristo Range. This was the terminus of the Denver & Rio Grande railroad at that time, and from there he rode the stagecoach to Lake City, almost 200 miles to the west and across two mountain ranges.

Here Darley describes the stage road, which descended precipitously from Slumgullion Pass west of the Continental Divide into the high valley where Lake City is located:

*George M. Darley, Presbyterian Minister*

> It was a long, hard stage ride from La Veta into the San Juan country. During the day the grandeur of the scenery would interest passengers, but as soon as the stage struck the "Slumgullion Road" even old-timers would join the freighters in swearing at each other to "pull off the road." On this road there was a drop of several thousand feet in about twelve miles, and a few miles of that was corduroy. The freighters claimed that "every ten feet there was a stone projecting from six to eighteen inches, and frequently on the opposite side a hole from six to eighteen inches deep, with a stump in the middle."

Even today this route has the steepest grade of any continuously paved road in Colorado, and all roads ended at Lake City. As Darley put it, "To go beyond Lake City meant to go where there were no bridges across streams and, in some directions, no wagon roads—only trails through the greater part of the San Juan, and often they were very rough, while the distance between cabins was so great that frequently the missionary had to sleep on the ground." Darley made his headquarters in the little boom town of Lake City and immediately set to work to establish a Presbyterian church there. He reported that, "In the spring of 1876 there was not a church building on the Pacific slope in Colorado."

Like many mountain missionaries before and since, Darley attracted an audience by going to the places where he knew that idle men could be found. Most of the time this meant entering the saloons and gambling halls which were the center of social life in the boom towns.

When entering the camps where no religious services had been held, I invariably went to the right place to find an audience, and in every case was courteously and kindly received and generally told: "Just wait, Brother Darley, until the games can be stopped, and we will give you a chance at the boys." It was not always an easy matter to stop the games. Winners were usually willing, while the losers were not. But as soon as the games closed then roulette, keno, poker, and faro would give place for a time to the Gospel.

A more convenient pulpit than a faro table could not be found, nor a more respectful and intelligent audience. In what occasional singing we did have, men with trained voices, rich and sweet, would sing without books those grand old hymns: "Jesus, Lover of My Soul" and "Rock of Ages, Cleft for Me." With bowed heads they listened to the prayer, often with tears in their eyes for the "old, old story" being told as they had heard it "back East," while sitting in a pew beside father, mother, or fond wife and dear children. The contrast was as great between the Eastern pew and Western beer kegs, whisky barrels, and chairs, as it was between the Eastern pulpit and a Western faro table, behind which the minister stood, but the Christ presented was the same—and those men's souls were as dear to the Savior.

Darley's general assessment of the men in those camps was that they were intelligent and friendly. He found many who had been taught sound spiritual values in Eastern homes by religious parents. Yet in the free-wheeling and permissive environment of the mining camps, he noticed that even men from the best homes would often gravitate toward the gambling halls that were common in all the camps. They

*Faro table typical of the gambling halls at Lake City, Colorado, around 1876.*
Reprinted from Darley (1899), 48.

claimed they only wanted to see what was going on inside, rather than desiring to participate, but despite their best intentions they often were caught in the addictive excitement of the games. Here Darley describes one encounter he had with a young prospector he met just outside a gaming establishment:

> I said to a young man fresh from the East, as I met him at the door of a large gambling hall: "Were you in the habit of entering such houses in the East?" He answered: "I was never in a saloon or gambling house in my life until I came to this camp. My folks would be ashamed of me if they knew I frequented such places." Having hold of his hand, and the light shining in our faces, I said: "Should you be any less of a man out West than you were back East?" By the flash of his eye and the color in his face I saw that he was offended, but I held his hand and kept looking him in the eye. Finally he dropped his head and said: "I ought not to be."

Several times Darley was asked why he associated directly with so many "sporting men and fast women." The more sanctimonious people in the community believed that such associations reflected badly on a minister's character. But he always tried to follow the example of Jesus, who became the friend of "publicans and sinners." Darley replied, "If I could not know and, so far as necessary, associate with all classes, I was not the man for the place." And Darley *was* the right man for the place!

He was called upon frequently to officiate at funeral services, and it was his policy to go wherever he was requested in order to minister to people's needs. It was only as a result of his relationships with all classes of people, and his reputation as an honest and caring preacher, that a funeral like the one described below took place:

> When asked, "Will you come to Magg Hartman's house and preach her funeral sermon?" I consented, because I believed it my duty to go wherever I was asked for the purpose of conducting funeral services. Magg Hartman lived in "Hell's Acre," a part of the new mining camp largely given to the sporting class. This part of the camp was well named "Hell's Acre" for the first part of the name was about all that was ever raised on that acre. As I entered the house a very tall, well-known character who was sitting on the floor rose and said as he took my hand: "Well, Parson, this is the way we all go." I replied: "Yes, we all must die, but it depends on how we have lived and in whom we have believed as to the place we go when we die." "I guess

that is so," said my tall friend, for the man was a friend in the way of "backing the Parson" financially and by being accommodating in various ways.

I then stepped to the side of the coffin and looked at Magg Hartman's more than ordinary face, for few faces were more remarkable and few lives had been stranger than that of this many-sided woman. As the "girls" came in from the dance halls I took each one by the hand and spoke a kind word. When all was ready for the funeral service I noticed a strained attempt on their faces to "take it" which plainly said: "You hold a full hand now, so just wade in." Before the first eleven verses of the eighth chapter of St. John had been read, arms were unfolded and the strained look began to leave their faces, and as words void of severity were spoken tears began filling their eyes. Soon every head was bowed and, had I not witnessed such scenes before, I might have believed every one would leave the paths of sin and seek a better life.

After the pall-bearers had fastened the top on the coffin, one of the girls asked if I would go with them to the cemetery. Her request was granted. Who can tell what impressions the reading of God's Word and the funeral sermon made upon the minds and hearts of those outcasts of society, many of them mere girls? Men who have seen much of life know that there are thousands of bleeding, aching and sorrowing hearts that are struggling against the terrible current of prejudice and cold-heartedness that is so prevalent—battling hard against the sense of shame in their own hearts and against the powers of a cold world—traveling in the most lonely of life's paths without one kind word to cheer, without one glimmer of light to guide their lonely footsteps until, discouraged, disheartened and crushed, words of deepest gloom fall from their lips.

Many are ready to cry: "It is their own fault. The young girl or young man ought to have remained at home and been good." Friends, how do you know that it is their own fault? Who told you so? What means have you of knowing so much? Be honest and acknowledge that you are ignorant regarding their temptations, surroundings, education and peculiar temperaments, the promises made them and broken—made by those you are pleased to take by the hand. Then try to have enough Christian charity and hard common sense to keep you from kicking the fallen. It is well for the fallen that there are those on earth, as well as in Heaven, who can be "touched with the feeling of their infirmities."

On another occasion Darley was called to the funeral of a notorious faro dealer who had been the proprietor of the largest dance hall in the area. Here he describes their attempt to have a decent service:

> When it was known that Ben House had died at the San Juan Central, a large adobe dance hall, many said: "Ben was one of the best-hearted boys in the camp." Among those generally called the "boys" a feeling existed that, Ben having been engaged in a public business—although the kind of place in which he died was not in keeping with a great display at his funeral—the stores ought to be closed during the services, and that "just as good a send off ought to be given Ben as possible."
>
> After most of the preliminaries had been arranged, Big Hank, one of Ben's intimate friends, came and stood by the remains, and as tears coursed down his cheeks he gave me a very glowing description of the departed. What nerve, what generosity, how no man could ever get Ben to go back on a friend, no matter how tight a place that friend was in. This eulogy was interspersed with all the oaths Big Hank could call to mind, just to be emphatic.
>
> As he finished eulogizing his dead friend, I noticed two "girls" from one of the dance halls coming into the building. I knew they were coming to pay their respects to Ben. One was a tall woman, known as Sorrel Top, on account of the color of her hair, and the other was a short, thick-set Mexican. To my surprise Big Hank was angry and would not permit either of the girls to look at Ben. Turning to me, he said: "I tell you, Mr. Darley, we are going to have a decent funeral out of this, and none of that crowd can come near Ben now." But I differed with him and sent him to get something that was needed. While he was away I invited both girls to look at Ben. They were not devoid of feeling or tenderness. The woman's heart was not entirely gone, and a few kind words were appreciated.

Darley kept a pastoral register in his notebook during this period, and it listed many deaths and funerals at which he presided during his first year in the mountains. Saloon keeper George Elwood was killed, and Luther Ray was murdered in a gambling hall. Charles C. Curtis died in his cabin during an avalanche. Alfred Shepherd died from exposure in a storm. Harry Pierce was killed by a premature blast in the Ula mine. John Furgerson was killed by a rock slide. Jackson Gregory and Newton N. Lytle died near the Old Dolly Varden Trail on Engineer Mountain when they were caught in an avalanche. Donald Robertson froze to death at night during a blizzard. Here Darley recounts a somewhat typical scene at a mountain funeral.

> During my varied experience in Colorado I have often officiated at funerals very different in appearance. A rough box holds the body and an old wagon is the hearse, the mourners and minister follow on foot. When the place of burial is reached, the hole in the ground is uneven in width, and boulders project on the sides. When we attempt to let down the box, the grave is too small, so we lift it out and enlarge the grave. Finally the body is laid to rest, as the wind sighs among the tree tops and the mountains receive to their arms another body dear to someone.

Living in the mountains during those days was a dangerous occupation, but most of the people were willing to take chances in the hope of striking it rich. Braving the rugged conditions of wilderness life and taking chances would also come to describe the itinerant preacher in the mountains. Darley commented that, "In the seventies many difficulties had to be faced in the San Juan that were more than the average minister cared to face then, or would care to face now." Here he describes his struggle to reach one preaching appointment at a remote mine:

> Before a minister can be made instrumental in reaching godless men, they must first be convinced that he is in earnest, not only in what he says but in all he does. One Sunday morning some friends said: "Mr. Darley, we hope you won't walk to the mine today." Over eighteen inches of snow had fallen, and the wind was blowing. I replied: "I must not miss my appointment." After a hearty dinner I changed my pulpit suit for one adapted to mountain trips and put on boots to match. It took nearly three hours to walk to the mine. The road was up grade all the way and in many places the snow was waist deep. Only one man was in the large room where services were held. He looked surprised and said: "We did not expect you today." He started to the bunk houses and soon the men came wallowing through the snow. Although tired, it was a treat for me to see the earnest look of inquiry on those stern, weather-beaten, manly faces. Afterwards the superintendent told me my walking to the mine that Sunday did great good. The men said: "That preacher must be in earnest, or he would not have walked up here after such a storm."

Since there were no established roads, hiking the mountain trails became the primary mode of transportation. As Darley put it, "During these years the few ministers who went to the front found no palace cars in which to ride and seldom a horse to mount. Walking was reasonably good and fashionable. Miner, prospector, merchant and preacher were privileged to walk." In the snowy winter months, Darley would wade through waist-deep snow as he traveled from place to place. He sent a description of one of his early journeys across the mountains to Sheldon Jackson, who published the following account in *The Rocky Mountain Presbyterian* newspaper:

> Darley started out to cross the mountains during a snow storm, and he finally reached a miner's cabin where the family insisted he stay the night with them. At four o'clock the next morning he began climbing toward the Continental Divide. After an hour he spotted another cabin, and he was given some breakfast. While there, Gus Talbot, who carried the mail over the mountains on snow shoes, came along with the mail. He had traveled sixteen miles since one o'clock that morning. They decided to travel together and by seven o'clock they had reached Burrows Park at about ten thousand feet above sea level. A number of miners were waiting there for the storm to pass, and none of them dared make the attempt. The mail carrier was determined to proceed, and he said: "Darley, I have carried the mail across here for years. Again and again have I crossed when I could not see as far as the point of my snow shoe. You have faced

*George M. Darley (right) and a traveling companion crossing the snowy ranges of the San Juan Mountains on "snow shoes" in the late 1870s.*
Reprinted from Darley (1899), 138.

the storm twenty-two miles yesterday; dare you face it twenty-three miles farther with me?"

With the calmness of men who understood the perils before them, they started—Gus Talbot with forty pounds of mail on his back and Mr. Darley with his blankets. Three miles brought them above timber line. The snow clouds drifted and surged around them. Every landmark was hidden. It seemed as if they were off in space with nothing in sight except the snow at their feet. On they plunged into that space, every few minutes stopping to gain breath.

At length they knew that they were descending, and supposed that they had turned the summit. But soon their hopes were dashed by coming to an ascent again. Knowing that something was wrong, they turned to the left, and crossed their own track, and the horrible suspicion began to draw upon them that they were lost. For three hours they had been plunging forward, unable to see anything before them. Fifteen minutes later and they again crossed their track, and the dread suspicion became a certainty. They were lost.

Oh that the clouds would open one half second so they could catch a glimpse of some landmark! But the impenetrable clouds still enveloped them. Knowing their only hope was to descend, they turned in their tracks and started downward. Soon they were conscious of a rapid descent, when all at once the mail carrier dropped from view— gone over a precipice! With horror, Mr. Darley sprang to one side as a great cake of snow gave way under his feet and followed the mail carrier below.

For a moment he seemed paralyzed; his heart seemed to cease to beat. Gathering up his consciousness, he at once started to the rescue. Groping his way around to the base of the cliff he found Mr. Talbot crawling out of the snow with the mail bags still on his back. The snow had broken his fall and saved his life. With great thankfulness they started on again. Soon a dim, dark line was seen below them, and they had reached the timber line.

With renewed energy they pressed forward and were soon sheltered from the storm in the pines, under which they lunched on a couple of biscuits. Half an hour later they reached the mining town of Animas Forks. Silverton was still fourteen miles away, and their trail led across the track of an avalanche. But so much greater were the dangers through which they had passed, that the rest of the way seemed easy. After a good meal they started down the Animas and made Silverton that night.

The next day Gus Talbot, the plucky mail carrier, told the people that they could "tie to George M. Darley, for out of more than one hundred men he had piloted across the range, the Presbyterian preacher was the only one that had the grit to keep with him all the way."

We who are on the frontier know that if the church would do her duty and give the Gospel to the regions beyond now, as in the days of the apostles and martyrs, some of her ministers must face physical hardships and sufferings. The men that observe the wind and regard the clouds and consult their comfort are not the men for the front. We need sterner material. We need men that can endure hardness, face dangers, take chances, attempting seeming impossibilities, not counting even their lives dear unto them, if thereby the church can be advanced. All honor to the pioneers of the church!

It was not until a year later that George Darley learned the real reason why he had been spared during that fearful experience in the blizzard crossing the Continental Divide. Some young men might have attributed their survival to physical endurance, strength, courage, determination, or even pure luck. But Darley later discovered that a little old lady had saved his life that night:

In all my varied experience I never had my heart so touched as it was by the recital of an old lady concerning her deep anxiety and all-night and all-day prayer for my safety. She was a quiet, unassuming, God-fearing woman, not easily approached, said little to anyone and seldom went anywhere except to church. I was making pastoral calls and had been in her home but a short time when tears came to her eyes as she asked: "Do you remember the terrible snow storm that swept over this San Juan country about a year ago?" I replied I had good reasons for remembering it, because it was the trip with Gus Talbot when we almost perished. "So have I," she said. "You know you gave notice in church that you would be absent the next Sunday, that you were going to Silverton to preach and intended to organize a church. I saw you ride by and knew you expected to go as far as Burrows Park, then snow-shoe it over the range.

You know I was the first white woman in all this region and, having lived several years among these mountains, I can tell by the way the clouds hang round the high peaks when there is going to be one of those terrible storms, and I knew by the way the clouds were gathering that before you reached Silverton the storm would overtake you. I knew your disposition so well, and from what I have often heard about you, I knew you would either get to Silverton or die on the range. So when night came and, with the darkness, that terrible storm, I prayed for you all that night and all the next day, for the storm still raged, and I knew you were in it somewhere on the range.

As soon as I could control my feelings sufficiently to speak without showing what some men call weakness, I said: "Now I know why I lived through that fearful storm."

The first church built on the western side of Colorado's Continental Divide was the Presbyterian church in Lake City, dedicated on November 19, 1876—just five months from the time it was initially organized. George Darley had the honor of being the first to pioneer this rugged area and to establish the first outpost of Christianity there. He later commented,

In no region can we find men who are so indifferent to religious influence as in the new mining camps. Yet this class like to see improvements in the camp, and often lend a helping hand. After our church was built in Lake City, saint and sinner expressed themselves as being very proud of it, and showed their appreciation by attending services and paying for their preaching...No class of men knew better how to treat a minister they liked in a royal manner than the men

*The first church built on the western slope of Colorado's Continental Divide, Lake City Presbyterian Church, 1876.*
Reprinted from Darley (1899), 16.

who went into southwestern Colorado during the great San Juan excitement of '75, '76 and '77.

During Darley's travels throughout the mountains, the basic comforts of civilized life were hard to come by. After arriving in one remote camp, he went in search of a place to clean up before preaching to the miners. Here he describes his search for a decent place to get a shave:

> After a night's rest and a warm breakfast I concluded, before visiting the people, to try to find someone who would either shave me or loan me a razor. Among the log cabins was one larger than the others, with the familiar sign over the door: "Saloon." As I drew near I asked a man if he knew where I could get shaved. "Yes," he said, "You can get shaved in a little room in the back end of that saloon." I walked in and through to the little room, and sure enough there was a box upon another box, with a board nailed to it at about the right slant for a barber's chair. In front of this fix-up was a mirror, some bottles, and a few razors. Four men were playing poker. The room being about eight by ten feet, we were a little crowded for space, but that was the least of my troubles.

> When I looked at the man who did the shaving I confess that, if the four better-looking men who were gambling had not been in the room, he would not have shaved me. If whisky ever blossomed in full, it was on that man's face. He apologized for his looks by saying that he was "just recovering from a very severe attack of erysipelas." Did it not sound harsh, I should say from a very severe spell of the "jimjams." His razor was dull and his hand was quite unsteady. Finally he finished a twenty-five cent job of scraping. I paid the bill, told the crowd there would be preaching somewhere in town that evening, invited all to come, and walked out. That night I preached to a fair-sized audience and secured signers to a petition for a church organization.

There were so many growing camps throughout the region, and each of them attracted people who needed his ministry. In the summer of 1877, Sheldon Jackson joined Darley for a trek through the San Juans to the booming town of Ouray, Colorado. Here is Jackson's published account of that journey from *The Rocky Mountain Presbyterian*:

> After a pleasant Sabbath spent with the little church at Lake City, Mr. Darley and myself started on Monday morning for Ouray. We rode up the cañon of Henson Creek for ten miles, between lofty

rock walls from 100 to 1,000 feet high. By noon we were at Capitol. After a good dinner, we shouldered our blankets and provisions and started on foot up the cañon. All along were beautiful waterfalls and cascades a thousand feet high. Here and there we passed where the avalanche had cut a broad swath down the mountainside, carrying away the trees, both stumps and limbs. Five miles up, at the edge of the snow line, we came to a new log cabin built by Messrs. Smith and Harris. Here we camped for the night.

About sundown the clouds began to gather and the snow to fall, and with it fell our hopes of crossing. But earnest prayer was made that He who causes the elements to do His bidding should so control them that we could get across. Soon the clouds floated away and the sky was clear again.

Our blankets were spread upon a pile of shingles and I was soon sleeping soundly. Mr. Darley, who could not sleep, kept the fire burning and amused himself by throwing chips at the chipmunks that played around the floor and ran over our beds. At 2 AM he woke me with the announcement that breakfast was ready. Eating breakfast of bacon, biscuit and coffee, by half-past three we were on our way to get over the crust before the morning sun should soften it.

We floundered over the fallen timber in the dark, felt our way over logs across streams or waded them, and when boots and socks were thoroughly wet, we found a grim satisfaction in wading all subsequent streams rather than balance on an uncertain log. In an hour we were at timber line, or an elevation where timber ceases to grow. We now started zigzag up the vast field of frozen snow and ice. The air grew rarer and rarer, and breathing became more and more difficult.

The wet boots became frozen and the wet feet ached as if they were freezing too. Up and still up we went. At each step the heel of the boot was driven firmly into the frozen snow, each one trying to step in the dent made by the one who preceded him. A misstep or slip would send the unlucky traveler whirling down the snow-face of the mountain, to be dashed in pieces on the rocks below.

Every few steps, securing our heels in the snow, we would lie out at full length exhausted, heart thumping, nose bleeding, eyes running, and ears ringing. From near the summit a detached rock was sent whirling down the vast snow-field until a mile below it seemed like a top spinning on the floor.

Daylight was approaching and still we were painfully climbing, until, as the first rays of the morning sun were lighting up a hundred grand mountain peaks around, we gained the summit at 13,500 feet. And from that summit what a panorama greeted our eyes! On either side was Mt. Sickels and Engineer's Peak. Off to the north, the great Uncompahgre Peak, 14,235 feet high, was head and shoulders above his fellows. Far away to the west, in the dim blue distance, was a wilderness of peaks, and all covered with snow, with the exception of some rocks too steep for the snow to lie upon. Nothing but snow was visible—a Canadian January scene in the middle of June.

But it was too cold to tarry and we were soon plunging down the western face of the mountain. Where it was not too steep, we ran down the face of the snow, and where it was too steep for running, we would sit down and slide. And such a slide of a thousand feet at a breakneck speed might well be the great event of the season for the average schoolboy. Between running and sliding, we were down in twenty minutes, a distance that on the other side had cost us two hours of painful climbing, and were at the first cabin on the headwaters of the Uncompahgre River.

Without halting, we plunged down the cañon, as there was yet considerable snow to be crossed. The descent was rapid, and the trail bordered with a constant succession of waterfalls, any one of which would have repaid a trip of a hundred miles. Soon after reaching timber line the snow ran out, and we had a succession of dry ground, mud, and fording the mountain torrents. Down we went until we reached Poughkeepsie Creek, which through a wild and almost inaccessible cañon joins the Uncompahgre from the west.

Here we lost the trail and got off into the fallen timber. By the time the trail was found, my feet were so blistered from traveling in wet and at times frozen boots that I could go no farther. We were in the heart of the mountains, still ten miles from town. It was decided that Mr. Darley should leave the provisions and blankets with me, and then push on to Ouray and send back a horse to carry me in. Building a fire and spreading the blankets, I went to sleep with my feet drying at the fire.

Four hours passed, and Mr. Darley returned without the horse. Shortly after leaving me, he had again become lost, and after wandering around, found himself at the bottom of a deep cañon where the water of the mountain torrent filled from rock to rock, shutting off all further progress. To extricate himself from that gorge, he had

*Miners gathered for preaching in a remote San Juan Mountain camp.*
Reprinted from Darley (1899), 54.

climbed great pine trees that, like stairs, enabled him to get from one rock ledge to another. On his return, he had met a miner going to Ouray, and being too exhausted to walk with him, had sent a note informing the Presbyterians of our situation.

After a good rest in camp, a burro pack train came along and we hired our passage into Ouray on the same kind of animal that the Savior made His triumphal entry into Jerusalem. So, mounting a burro without saddle or bridle, we started for town. The trail led up and down mountainsides so steep that, going up, we had great difficulty keeping from sliding off behind, and going down, we felt like bracing with our feet behind the animal's ears, and along the edge of precipices, where the giving away of a stone could send both animal and rider into the foaming river a thousand feet below. Just before reaching the village, we met a party with horses and provisions coming to our relief, and soon after we were safe among friends. An appointment was made for preaching, and the evening of June 13th, after the sermon, the First Presbyterian Church of Ouray was organized.

The second church to be built on the Western Slope of the Colorado Rockies was the Presbyterian Church in Ouray, dedicated on October 14, 1877. Darley could say, "without fear of contradiction, that in no other frontier town in Colorado could the same amount of money be

113

raised more easily than that so cheerfully given by the citizens of that camp for the erection of their first house of worship."

Darley had proved himself to be a man's man, as well as an honest and caring minister. He earned the respect and admiration of the rough men in the mountains. In later years Darley remembered how the old-timers often spoke of a particularly daring 125-mile journey he made over the San Juans in just five days—a feat that few could match. He had reached Ouray with swollen limbs, and was almost completely exhausted. Two of the miners brought him to their cabin and found a bottle of arnica, which they applied to revive his legs and arms. Hardly able to walk, he insisted on preaching to a group of men who had gathered there. Before his return journey, the men pleaded with him not to cross Engineer Mountain, since it was snowing hard by that time in Ouray. Darley reflected, "Like some other young men who lived in the San Juan at that time, my bump of caution was not very well-developed, so I started and found nearly four feet of fresh snow above timber line." Darley gained a reputation as a courageous and intrepid "brother" to that rugged breed of men in the mountains.

Throughout his ministry, Darley continued to hold a high opinion of the people in the mountains, despite their faults and foibles.

> Association with all classes during the San Juan excitement taught me that many of the reckless class, notwithstanding their faults, were neither narrow-minded nor selfish. Though they gave from impulse rather than principle, they were often very generous...After preaching, a pleasant-looking man took my hand and said, "Come again." I felt something soft, and held to it. After taking a few steps I examined what was in my hand and found a twenty-dollar bill. Since then I have preached in wealthy churches without receiving anything more than expressions of appreciation. One peculiarity about drinking men in "live" mining camps is their sense of honor when dealing with a minister. They insist on paying for their preaching and for funeral services. Often when refusing to accept money for officiating at a funeral, men have said: "Parson, you can't live without money any more than the rest of us."

As a result of almost a decade of rough service in the mountains, George Darley's health began to suffer and he was forced to retreat to lower elevations for a well-deserved rest. While he was packing his few household goods to leave his mountain home, he received a visit from two of his mining friends.

Without any preliminaries one of them began piling up silver dollars and five-dollar bills on a little table. When the money was counted, the one who brought it said: "Mr. Darley, there is one hundred and thirty-seven dollars from the boys—not one cent is from a church member. You have given us hell for five years, but you have always given it to us in the teeth. You have been kind to us when we were sick, and never said one word against the dead. We are sorry you are going away and this is to show our appreciation."

George M. Darley left the mountains, but he remained active in ministry in Colorado. He began serving the Presbyterian Church at Del Norte, and in 1883 he organized the "Presbyterian College of the Southwest" there. His ministry in the Rocky Mountains extended for forty-five years.

# The Gunnison Country
# and into Wyoming

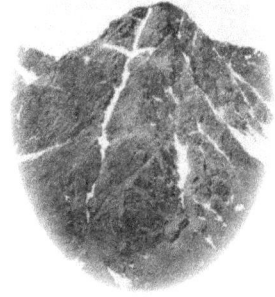

The Gunnison country was situated north of the San Juan Mountains, and it was the next to experience a mining boom around 1877. By 1881 the Denver & Rio Grande Railroad had also reached Gunnison, and the introduction of this new transportation infrastructure seemed to accelerate the life cycle of the region. The miners and ranchers welcomed the railroad, which contributed to the rapid growth and exploitation of the area. But Gunnison was to experience one of the fastest boom and bust cycles anywhere. Within five or six years of the arrival of the miners and railroads, the relatively low grade ores had been exhausted and half the population left the area using the same railway on which they had arrived.

Congregationalist minister Roselle T. Cross came to Colorado in 1876 at the request of the Home Mission Board, serving churches in Colorado Springs, Pueblo, and Denver for several years. He was an amateur geologist who organized boys clubs for exploring the foothills of the Rocky Mountains. His club in Colorado Springs is credited with the 1880 discovery of the famous "Cave of the Winds." During that same year, R.T. Cross made a spiritual exploring trip through the Gunnison country as well.

In the summer of 1880 there was a great rush to what was called the Gunnison. The superintendent asked this writer to go and supply the churches. Leaving home at eleven PM and passing through the Grand Cañon of the Arkansas in the night, he reached South Arkansas, now

117

Salida, at six AM. This was not far from the point which, three years before, it had taken our camping party seven days to reach. It was a long day's journey by stage of sixty miles over the Continental Divide to Gunnison City. Two men on the stage opened the day's ride with considerable profanity. One of them learned that their fellow passenger was a clergyman, and he whispered something to his companion, of which the only word the pastor caught was "preacher." They did not swear any after that.

In going down the other side, the pastor had his first experience riding down a mountain road with six horses running at full speed. The curves were sharp and descent rapid, but the roadbed was good and there was nothing to do but trust in a strong brake, a skillful driver, and a good Providence, and lean back and enjoy it. At the first halt on the other side to change horses, the tires of the hind wheels were hissing hot, so closely had the brake been applied. The forty mile ride from the summit to Gunnison was through a lovely valley, but it was a rough and dusty ride. At one point among the thick bushes beside the road, five highwaymen or road agents were lying in wait for the stage after it had passed! Fortunately it was nearly two hours ahead of its usual time.

Thirty miles more of staging the next day brought us to Crested Butte, another point where a church had been organized. Making this place headquarters, we walked the next day to Ruby Camp where some 2,000 people were living in log cabins and tents at an altitude of 10,000 feet, and where sixty feet of snow were said to

*A church building at Ruby Camp, Colorado, in 1882.*
Courtesy of Denver Public Library Western History Collection: X-9554.

have fallen the previous winter. Securing the use of a large tent, we got some handbills printed announcing services on Sunday, and on Saturday we left them at all the houses, tents, stores, and saloons. Going to the tent Sunday morning, horses were found stabled in it. The owner took them out, and returning after breakfast the preacher found it full of smoke from a fire built on the ground to disinfect the tent. He borrowed lumber and blocks, got some young men to help him, and prepared seats. A steel bar vigorously pounded called the people together. A large congregation of men, with only three or four women, listened to the sermon. The Christian people remained after the service and discussed the question of a church organization.

Sixteen miles of horseback riding and walking brought the preacher to Gothic in time for an evening service with the new church at that place. That town is now almost deserted, and the church long ago became extinct. The location of the place from a scenic point of view was one of the grandest in the Rocky Mountains. In riding eight miles the next day from Gothic to Rock Creek, we passed five embryo towns. It seemed as though every man who could find a tolerably level forty acre lot laid out a town on paper. On the next Sunday, after preaching again at Gothic, he walked to Crested Butte to preach in the evening. The preacher had to pull off his boots to wade through the snow-cold waters of Snake River. At Crested Butte there was some excellent material in the church, and it is now the only church of its order left in that region, as Crested Butte proved to be the only permanent town of any consequence.

Another Congregational clergyman, Sherlock Bristol, tells the story of his meeting with a small group of miners who were not enamoured with preachers and wanted to have some fun at his expense. Here is his description of what happened during this encounter:

The next day we crossed the river on an immense pine tree which had fallen across the stream. It was probably from 150 to 200 feet long and as we went across one at a time it swayed up and down in the middle perhaps five or six feet, and it made one's head swim to look down into the water ten or twelve feet deep, rushing beneath us. Passing a brush house, a couple of fellows just crawling out of their blankets hailed us. "Hallo! Just from God's country? Well, call in. We want to inquire about things." We stopped and after a while they proposed to show us some specimens of the gold they were taking from their mines nearby. He drew forth a shot bag partly filled with gold and we took it out in handfuls. It was mostly in lumps about as large as lead drops, or the size of kernels of corn, and bright and beautiful.

There occurred an encounter with a rough, of which I hesitate to write lest the reader should regard my action as savoring too much of the "Fighting Parson," and as being quite un-ministerial if not un-Christian. However, as it was more ludicrous than serious, I will give it for all it is worth and as it occurred. The owner of the adjoining claim came over the heap of boulders piled up between the two claims, and I was introduced as a preacher. "A minister!" said he, "A minister!" He despised ministers and church members. He would have some fun at their expense and have a ludicrous story to tell at the saloon. He was the one who organized a club at the bar, one of whose resolutions was to treat to a dose of mud any clergyman who should chance to come upon their bar!

Well, he mounted the pile of boulders, and swinging his hat he cried out: "Hear ye! Hear ye! O yes! O yes! Every miner quit his work! Hurry here! There is fun ahead! Come one! Come all!" Instantly, from up the river and down, the rockers ceased their rattle and the miners came vaulting over the piles of boulders, and in five minutes some thirty to fifty were on hand, with more coming. I suppose I could have got away by hard running if I had started quick enough. As the crowd gathered, a Dr. Weber begged them to spare me as his friend, but they wanted fun.

The bully seized my collar and said: "Enough of this gab! Dry up. Parson! I will show you how we do it!" So saying he gave me a violent jerk which brought my right hand against his neck, and my left hand grasped a handful of his shirt collar and vest, and perhaps some of the flabby flesh adjacent. There came over me a strange spasm of impulsive energy, giving me about thrice my ordinary strength, and his feet left the ground and he landed on his back in a puddle of water! What a shout went up from every miner's mouth—save one!

He sprang up, and seeing that I was in for it I took both of his hands, in wrestler's style, knocked his feet from under him and laid him on his back again! Jerking him up again, I threw him from me ten feet distant against a pile of rocks! I intended this should end it, but the wicked eye which looked at me as he was rising instantly changed my mind. I thought he might have a dirk or pistol and I resolved to shake that out of him quick, so I sprang like a cat upon him and

*The preacher's response to rough treatment in the mining camp.*
Reprinted from Bristol (1887), 176.

seizing him by the pants and collar, I gave him such a shaking up as made him limp as a dish rag. "Will you behave?" I asked energetically. Not answering, I started with him for the river. I repeated my question and emphasized it with a fresh shaking up. Meanwhile the crowd followed, making the woods ring with their laughter.

He finally cried out, "Enough, Parson!" and I threw him down saying, "The next minister who comes along here, you treat him decently." Wishing to get through the dirty job as soon as possible I now turned to the largest man among them, but he gracefully stepped back, bowed, and said, "No, thank you! You shall pass!" As no one else seemed disposed to try his hand at dirtying the minister's coat, I tried to resume my conversation with Dr. Weber as if nothing special had happened. He laughed and fairly roared, and so did the rest, even the members of that club. They wanted some fun and they had got it.

Dr. Weber introduced me to the miners, each by name, and soon we got into a lively conversation. They said they hoped I would not regard them as the worst of men, even if they were a little rough. Now the miners were eager to have me go to their tents and take dinner with them. And if I would preach to them the next Sabbath they would all turn out, and would help in the singing. They assured me the best of order would be maintained, and that the resolution to put ministers through an initiatory course of sprouts should thence onward be considered as antiquated and annulled.

121

During the mid-1880s mining was not the only "boom" activity that was taking place. This was also the era of the cowboys and "cattle kings" on the high prairies. Ranching had become big business during this time, and the cattle ranges extended throughout the western territories. Where there were people in need of ministry, the home missionaries were sure to follow—and some pastors tended to the spiritual needs of their "flocks" on the high plains. As a general rule, the cowboys were an isolated, independent-thinking lot, and it took more than mere words to win their approval. Here one new preacher on the cattle ranges of Wyoming shares his story of winning over the skeptics:

It was a typical Wyoming day in August. The air was crisp and cool and bracing. The stage left Cheyenne promptly at six in the morning. As one seated himself beside the driver on the high box, which is considered the choice place and must be reserved in advance, and breathed the ozone of the plains, a peculiar sense of exhilaration came over him. It was my first stage-ride in the Far West. I began to congratulate myself on the prospect of an enjoyable time. I have since learned, by long experience, that the best part of a stage ride is the first hour or two. After one has ridden all day and all night, and perhaps the greater part of the second day, the idea of enjoyment has departed. They change horses every fifteen or twenty miles, and the driver is relieved at nightfall by some one to take his place, but the unfortunate passenger who is booked to the end of the route gets no change. On this occasion it was about four in the afternoon on the second day that I arrived at my destination. I was covered with alkali dust, and must have looked as unlike a bishop as possible. As the stage halted and I alighted, I was cordially greeted by a man in his shirt-sleeves. He offered his services, and said he thought I looked like a parson. After a little conversation, I told him who I was.

"Why, are you the bishop? Well, I am delighted to see you. What can I do for you?" I asked him if he could tell me where my old friend from Missouri, Mr. Robinson, lived. "Do you mean Billy Robinson?" he asked. "Yes," I replied. "They used to call him 'William' back in Missouri, but that is the man."

"Oh yes," said he, "I know Billy Robinson well. In fact, I busted broncos for Billy for two years. Billy is a fine fellow. Everybody knows Billy. And so you are a friend of Billy Robinson! How glad he will be to see you! He lives about two miles out of town. He has a big ranch, and is getting rich. Bishop, if you will let me, I will be proud to take you out to Billy's place."

I thanked him for his offer. He then said, "I am sorry, Bishop, not to give you a carriage. It is a pity not to give a bishop a carriage, but there are no carriages here. This is a new town. But can you ride a bronco?" "Oh yes, thank you," I replied. "I was brought up on a farm and educated on a mule and am familiar with horses, and I think I can manage a bronco."

"Good," he said. "Now, Bishop, I have two broncos. One bucks pretty hard and the other bucks kind o' mild." "Well," said I, "Suppose you let me have the one that bucks kind of mild."

Accordingly, we were soon galloping towards Billy Robinson's ranch. My bronco proved to be literally a "mild" bucker, and only indulged that natural tendency on one occasion, when I jumped him over a pair of bars, and my valise, which I was holding in front, fell on his neck. As we reached the outskirts of the little village, I remember my new friend said to me:

"Say, Bishop, I want to put myself straight with you. I believe in a square deal. I don't want you to get the idea that I am one of your religious fellows, for I am not. I am a Bob Ingersoll man through and through, and all of us boys here are Bob Ingersoll men, and we take the *Boston Investigator*.* My name is Billy Bartlett, and I own this saloon here in town. When I saw you get out of the stage, I thought you looked sort o' lonesome-like, and made up my mind to give you the glad-hand."

I thanked him for his courtesy, and tried to set him at ease by assuring him that I did not think Mr. Ingersoll so bad a man after all, that I thought him a good citizen and a kind father, and believed he loved his fellow man. "But tell me, Mr. Bartlett," I continued, "What is the *Boston Investigator*? I have often heard of Boston, but never, until now, of the *Boston Investigator*."

"Ah," said he, "That is Bob's paper. It has lots of jokes in it, and Bob pokes fun at Moses and the Bible, and we boys all sit around the

---

* Robert G. Ingersoll was a lawyer and public orator who toured the nation speaking on a wide variety of subjects. In those days, attending lectures given by talented orators was a popular form of public entertainment, and Ingersoll spoke to packed houses across the country. He was the acknowledged king of American orators and became the friend of US Presidents, literary figures like Mark Twain and Walt Whitman, businessmen like Andrew Carnegie and Thomas Edison, as well as having a large popular following. He became well-known as an outspoken agnostic who would poke fun at orthodox Christian religion in his verbal and printed works. The Boston Investigator was a newspaper dedicated to "free thought" which printed many of Ingersoll's speeches.

stove at night and laugh." So the conversation went on. He reminded me that "back East" he used to go to church, and that his uncle was a preacher, but that he had not been to meetin' once since he came West, nearly ten years ago. "Why, Bishop," he added, "You are the first preacher that ever came to this town."

I assured him that, as the town was new and far distant from the railroad, the church was a little late in coming, but that I hoped some arrangement might be made to have regular services maintained.

Soon we came in sight of Mr. Robinson's ranch, and seeing a man coming out of the barn, Mr. Bartlett exclaimed: "There he is. That's Billy Robinson. Now, Bishop, you just keep this bronco and use him the rest of the day. I have no further use for him, and tonight you can ride him into church. Billy Robinson will want to show you his cattle and horses and sheep and his fine ranch and irrigating ditches, and then he will give you a good supper and bring you in to meetin'. So, if you will excuse me, Bishop, I will go back in town and round up all the boys."

"Oh, thank you very much," said I. "But I do not think that is at all necessary, Mr. Bartlett, for I sent your postmaster a number of printed notices announcing the service for this evening in the school-house. I also wrote him a polite note and asked him to be good enough to let all the people know of my coming in advance."

"Ah, but Bishop, that plan did not work at all. No doubt the post-master got your circulars, but he is the meanest Bob Ingersoll man in the whole business. He probably stuck all your posters in the stove. No, the people don't know you're coming. Why, I didn't even know it myself. So you must let me go, and I'll send out some cowboys on their broncos, and we'll round up every galoot in the country, and pack that schoolhouse for you."

With that remark he turned his horse around and was about to leave, when it occurred to me that I had made no provision for the music.

"Excuse me, Mr. Bartlett," I said, "But do you sing?"

"Now, Bishop," he replied, "Who gave me away? Who told you that I sing? You have caught right on to my racket. It just happens that I am a jo-dandy at singing, and I also play the fiddle and the organ."

"How fortunate I am," I remarked. "Then will you take charge of the music?" He demurred at first, and said he did not think a fellow of his kind was "fit for that business." But I insisted. I told him we would not try anything difficult, but simply have some old familiar hymns like "Rock of Ages" and "Jesus Lover of My Soul." At last he said: "Well, Bishop, if you say so, it is a go. I'll do my best."

After spending the rest of the day with Mr. Robinson, renewing the old associations and memories of our life in Missouri, and enjoying the excellent supper so hospitably provided for me, we rode back to the town. To my surprise, the schoolhouse was indeed crowded. Every available space in the little building was filled. Never in my life did I preach a sermon where I was given a more reverent and attentive hearing. As to Billy Bartlett, who presided at the organ, he sang, as his friends said, "like a bird." After the service he came up to me, and, with tears in his eyes, grasped my hand. With much emotion he thanked me, and said:

"Bishop, that talk will do us boys a world of good. That is the kind of stuff that we fellers need. Can't you stay over and give us another tomorrow night? There are some of the boys who couldn't get here tonight who would like to hear you. And are we never to have a church? Can't you send us a preacher? Bishop, if you will send us a

*St. John's Chapel, Shoshone Episcopal Mission, Wind River, Wyoming.*
Courtesy of Library of Congress Prints and Photographs Division.

preacher, all of us chaps will pitch in and support him and stand by him."

It was not long after this visit that I was able to secure a young man for that region who proved most acceptable. Nothing could have been more admirable than the manly spirit with which he threw himself into his work, and soon won the hearts of those sturdy pioneers, and I had the happiness to dedicate a seemly church which they so generously helped to build.

This story was told by Ethelbert Talbot, a young man who had served Episcopal churches in Missouri before being appointed the Missionary Bishop of Wyoming and Idaho in 1886. Some time after the events in this story, Talbot was called before a large missionary conference to give an impromptu account of the progress of his work. He began sharing this story, without realizing that a reporter from the *Washington Post* was copying every word.

Later Talbot was unaware that his account had been published in the *Denver Republican* and the *Rocky Mountain News*, as well as other papers across the West. When he next visited his friends in Wyoming, he noticed the newspaper clipping tacked to the wall of Billy Robinson's cabin. Robinson told him, "That speech of yours has been read from the Atlantic to the Pacific. Billy Bartlett has his in a frame and says he wouldn't take a thousand dollars for it."

Talbot would go on to establish almost forty churches and schools in the West during his ministry, and we will hear more of his adventures in the following chapter.

# Talbot's Adventures in Idaho

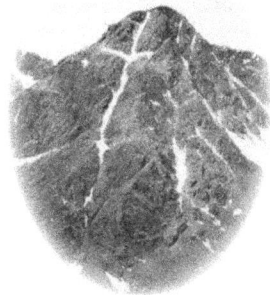

Ethelbert Talbot received a telegram in October 1886 which appointed him to lead the Episcopal missionary efforts in Wyoming and Idaho, serving as Daniel Tuttle's replacement after he took his new post as Bishop of Missouri. At Talbot's installment ceremony there was a man whose son lived in Cheyenne, Wyoming, and he told Talbot, "Cheyenne is the richest town of its size in the whole world today." This town had been the headquarters for some of the great cattle kings, but the severe winter of 1886-1887 almost wiped out the cattle population. It took years for Wyoming to recover from these losses, so its economy was quite depressed at the time of Talbot's arrival.

The blizzards that raged in Wyoming had not affected Idaho quite as severely. Talbot spent the summer months touring the mining camps of Idaho, holding church services wherever he could gather a crowd. He visited towns with names like Chalice, Bay Horse, Clayton, Silver City, Idaho City, Placerville, Murray, Wallace, Wardner, and many others. His goal was to reach every camp at least once each year, and members in some of the camps built churches for regular meetings when they could support a local pastor. Here Talbot describes the sensation caused by the arrival of a preacher in some of the remote mountain areas:

*Ethelbert Talbot,*
*Episcopal Minister*

In those days the visit of a bishop was an occasion of unusual inter-est. The camps, as a rule, were far from a railroad, and the annual visit of the bishop brought into the life of the place a new interest, es-pecially since the bishop was the only minister of any religious body who visited the settlement from year to year. If any of the young people were looking forward to being married, the important ques-tion was, "When is the Bishop coming?" It was often possible to time the event as to have it coincide with his visit, and hence it was desir-able that the date of his coming should be widely published in the local papers some months in advance. Then there were the children to be baptized, and a feast was generally given and the neighbors invited to be present.

Like those before him, Talbot was impressed with the character of the people on the frontier. He found that life in the wilderness seemed to develop a "high type of manhood quite unusual elsewhere." Even though the people were not affiliated with a specific church, they saw the need for decency and morality, and generally they were staunch supporters of the visiting ministers. He commented:

My readers may find themselves wondering whether there is much opportunity in the Western mining camp for religion and the church. One must frankly admit that the life of the average miner is a pecu-liarly hard one. From the necessity of the case the mines must run on Sunday as well as every other day, otherwise the water would flow in and destroy in one day the labor of weeks. The pumps must be kept going. When Sunday comes, therefore, it finds one-half of the men hard at work, and the other half must rest from their labors.

When they have an evening off, if it happens to be Sunday, many of them will go to church, and, when there, no one is more appreciative and attentive than the miner. The minister finds abundant opportu-nity to exercise his gifts of service in dealing with him individually, in learning to know when he is accessible and where. Providing him with a bright, attractive reading room, where the papers and maga-zines can be read, and where a game of pool, of billiards, or cards, or checkers can be innocently indulged in. Helping to provide a simple hospital where he can be cared for when sick or wounded. There is not only an abundant opportunity, but often a most pathetic need.

If the minister of Christ is to be of any real help to men in such environments, he must first of all be a manly man with a genius for service born of loving sympathy. It is the personal rather than the official touch that wins. To do men good they must be met on their own ground. It is not a loss of dignity, but the truest dignity, to identify one's self with the sorrows, anxieties, and even with the joys of those whom it is an honor to serve just because they are men.

This is exactly the kind of minister that Ethelbert Talbot proved to be among the mountain mining camps. He was not afraid to go into the saloons and dance halls to talk with the men and women there. Other preachers who held what they called "higher standards" would not sully their reputations by entering any of these "dens of iniquity," but their so-called ministries were not as effective and were usually cut short. Here Talbot shares one of his experiences in a remote mining camp, and tells the sad tale of another minister who could not adapt to its rugged lifestyle.

I recall very vividly my first visit to a certain mining camp. It involved a stage ride of seventy-five miles over a rough mountain road. I reached the place about sundown on Friday evening. As I alighted from the stagecoach in front of the hotel, a little man demurely presented himself. He extended his hand and asked: "Is this the Bishop?"

"Yes," I replied. "Well, Bishop, I am Brother May, the new minister. I arrived only yesterday. I am so glad to see you, Bishop, for this is the most God-forsaken hole I ever struck."

"Oh, well, do not be discouraged, my good brother," I answered, "for, if it is such a place as you describe, you and I are much needed here, and we shall find plenty of work to do. I shall see you a little later, and we shall have a good talk."

So I passed on into the hotel. As I registered my name I noticed behind the counter all the attractive paraphernalia of a first-class saloon. I was dusty and tired and hungry. After having made myself somewhat presentable, I was soon eagerly paying my respects to the various dishes set before me in the dining room. Hunger is, indeed, the best sauce, and how I did relish the food in the mining camps after those stage rides over the mountains.

Dinner over, I returned to the hotel office. There I found Brother May awaiting me. I offered him a cigar, but he declined, with a look of some surprise that a bishop should be addicted to such a vice. I proposed a stroll up the cañon, for, after sitting on the stagecoach all day, I felt the need of a walk. Brother May was very communicative. He proceeded to tell me the story of his life. He said he had been living in San Francisco, that as a boy he had been apprenticed to a printer and had learned to set type, and might have done well, but had fallen into bad company and acquired the habit of drink. He had also been addicted to gambling, and that he had gone from bad to worse, until finally he had lost his position and his friends, and was an outcast. About that time there was a great revival in the city. He dropped in one night and became interested. He was gradually led to see the evil of his ways, and determined, with God's help, to lead a new life.

His conversion was so unmistakably the work of the Spirit of God that he felt he must consecrate the remainder of his days to the preaching of the Gospel. He was over thirty years of age, so he had no time to lose. The authorities of his church advised him to go to some theological seminary and prepare himself, but he told them that he knew the story of the cross and the love of God, and felt eager to proclaim the message to men. He asked for no large place, no important church. Indeed, he begged them to send him to the most neglected and sinful place to be found. "And so, Bishop," he said, "they sent me here. I came only yesterday. This is my first charge, and my church has certainly sent me to the most God-forsaken hole it could find."

I again tried to reassure him, and suggested that while, as he said, there were many saloons in the camp, it was not strange that such a situation should obtain, as there was no church and no minister before he came. I also expressed the hope that he would find the people kindly and warm-hearted and ready to cooperate with him in his efforts to do them good. But he evidently considered the prospect almost hopeless. We arranged that I should preach in the dance hall on the morning and evening of the approaching Sunday, and that he should hold forth at four o'clock in the afternoon. I told him that at my eleven o'clock service I should take pleasure in announcing his appointment, and also formally introduce him to his new flock, and ask him to say a word to them. This conversation took place Friday evening.

After enjoying a good, refreshing night's sleep, I found myself ready on Saturday morning to prepare for my Sunday duties. First of all, it was important to make sure of my congregation. I had come so far that I did not like the idea of a mere handful of women and children. I longed to get hold of the men. The main street seemed full of miners. It was payday and the place presented a sort of holiday appearance. It occurred to me that it was a good opportunity to become acquainted. As I walked down the street I saw advancing towards me an elegantly dressed gentleman with large diamonds shining upon his spotless linen. There were seven saloons in a row. As I drew near my handsome young friend, and was about to extend my hand, he surveyed me, concluded I was a parson, and might wish to interview him on some subject with which he was not familiar, and suddenly disappeared into one of the saloons. The experience was a little discomfiting, but I summoned up courage and determined to try again. The next man was in his shirt-sleeves, but had an open, frank countenance. I assumed as gracious and friendly an aspect as I could command, and was about to greet him, when he, too, darted into a saloon.

Twice defeated, I went back to the hotel, and asked Colonel Bums, the proprietor, to let me have some large writing paper. In a bold hand I wrote out a few notices. I announced that, as Bishop of Idaho, I had come to the camp and would preach the next morning, Sunday, at eleven o'clock, and in the evening at eight, and that both services would be in the dance hall. All were cordially invited to attend. Then the colonel let me have some tacks. I put up a notice at the hotel, at the post-office, at the large store, and at the blacksmith's shop. I then stood off and looked to see if anyone would read my notices. But, alas, there were already so many notices ahead of mine! One announced an exciting horse race Sunday afternoon, a second a mine to be sold, a third a ranch to be rented, etc. I soon discovered that my method of advertising was not likely to be successful. What more could I do?

As I walked by the saloons I observed that they were full of men. If only I had not been a bishop, I reflected, the problem would have been easy of solution, for then I could have gone in the saloons where the men were, and delivered my invitation in person. But how would it look for a bishop to visit such places even with the best of motives. At last I became desperate. I selected the first saloon in the row. I went in. I introduced myself to the proprietor. I told him I was the Bishop of Idaho, and had come in to pay my respects to him. He met me very cordially. "Why, Bishop, I am proud to know you. What will you have?"

I thanked him and told him I should be greatly indebted to him if he would kindly introduce me to those gentlemen, pointing to a large room back of the saloon, where the men were gathered. "Do you mean the boys in the pool-room?" he asked. "Yes, I presume I do." Thereupon he came out from behind the counter, put his arm in mine in a familiar way, as though we had been companions all our lives, and escorted me to the open doorway of the pool room.

"Boys," he cried out, "Hold up the game. Put up the chips just a minute. This is the Bishop right among us, and he wants to be introduced." With a politeness and courtesy which would have done credit to any drawing room in New York or Boston or Philadelphia, the men rose from their seats and welcomed me. I said, briefly: "Excuse me, gentlemen, I do not wish to interfere with your pleasure or your amusement. I have just come in to pay my respects to you. I am the Bishop, and am going to hold services in the dance hall tomorrow morning at eleven and in the evening at eight, and I shall be very glad to see you there."

I remember that one of them, evidently speaking in a representative capacity, thanked me for letting them know, and asked me again the hour, and assured me they would all be present. In this way I visited all seven saloons in the row. Everywhere I was treated with the most respectful consideration, and I did not hear one word that could have offended the most delicate conscience. When I had completed the round I felt that I was reasonably sure of a goodly number of men as my hearers.

Coming out of one of the saloons I suddenly encountered on the street my little friend, Brother May, the new minister. He gave me a look of commingled surprise and pity, and with it a slight touch of scorn, but no words were exchanged between us. When, after my visitation of the saloons, I returned to my hotel, I found Brother May with his face buried in a newspaper. He hardly deigned to speak to me. I asked him some question. He hardly vouchsafed a reply. I tried him again. At last he put down his paper, and, looking at me with a much aggrieved expression, said: "Look here, Bishop, didn't I see you coming out of a saloon?"

"Yes, Brother May, you did, and if you had watched me you would have seen me coming out of seven." "Well," he continued, "All I have to say is I am sadly disappointed in you. My heart had gone out to you, and I was thanking God for sending you to this awful place, and now to think of a bishop going into one of those hells."

I tried to explain to my reverend little brother that I had visited more saloons that day than in all of the days of my life before, that I was not a drinking man, and regretted the evils of strong drink as much as he or any man could. But I had come to get hold of those men, that I only visited the camp one Sunday a year, while he would have an opportunity every week to talk to them. Gradually it dawned upon him that my act was, after all, susceptible of a charitable interpretation, though he could not justify it. Nor could he agree with me in thinking that my efforts to secure the presence of the men would prove successful, but felt sure they would not come out, no matter what they promised—in short, that I had hopelessly impaired my influence with them. I could only ask him to wait and see. It was clearly evident that Brother May's faith in me had been subjected to a severe test, and had almost reached the breaking point. His ideals of the episcopal office had received a terrible blow.

That evening we gathered together a few good people, and practised some familiar hymns. A young woman was found who played the little organ. The morning came, a bright and beautiful Sunday. As the hour of service approached, I could see that a great crowd was gathering. I had already put on my robes, and was seated on the platform of the dance hall, where also the organ and the choir were placed. As the men filed in, they occupied every available space. I invited some to sit on the edge of the high platform. Others took advantage of the fact that the windows were opened, and stationed themselves there. A large number had to stand near the doorway.

From the beginning to the close of the service a hushed and entirely reverential demeanor characterized the assembly. They listened most patiently to all I had to say. There was something peculiarly solemnizing and inspiring in those manly and earnest faces as they seemed to respond to the appeal I was making. After I had finished the sermon I introduced Brother May. I told the men that while the church I had the honor to represent had not yet seen its way to send them a minister, yet I rejoiced that Brother May, representing another religious body, had come. I was glad to introduce him, and that he was to preach that afternoon at four. Then Brother May arose.

He was extremely short of stature, and had a long black mustache, curled up at the ends. He wore a bright green cutaway coat, a blue waistcoat, and red necktie. His boots had high heels, tapered after the cow-boy fashion. All eyes were instantly fastened upon him. A stillness that was painful fell upon the scene. Brother May stood near the platform. Instead of turning around and facing the people he stood sidewise, looking at them over his shoulder.

"Yes, brethren, as the Bishop has said, I am here, and I am here to stay. I have come to preach the Gospel, and my first sermon will be at four o'clock, here in this place. I want you all to be on hand, for God knows you need the Gospel. Just think of it, you have seven saloons here in this camp! Seven dens of hell! The fact is, this is the most God-forsaken hole I ever struck."

He sat down. There was no audible expression of dissent, but I could feel that my little brother had forfeited his opportunity to commend himself to the people. I was sorry. Another hymn was given out, and I was about to dismiss the congregation with my blessing when Colonel Bums, my landlord, stepped forward, and in a low but distinct voice said: "Bishop, haven't you forgot something?"

"What do you mean?" said I. "Why, the hat," replied the Colonel. "Excuse me," I answered, "you are right. I had quite forgotten the collection." "I thought so," said the Colonel. "It won't do to forget the hat, for yesterday was payday and these boys have a lot of money, and if you don't get it the saloons will, and it is much better for you to have it. Now, Bishop, if you will allow me, I will own that part of the business myself."

"Very good," I said. "Have you any suggestions, Colonel?"
"Only this, Bishop: I wish you would give us about five hymns."
"Five!" I exclaimed. "You surely do not mean five hymns."
"Yes, Bishop," he replied, "I want plenty of time. I do not want to be crowded. The boys are a little slow on collections."

I stepped over to the organ, and arranged with the young woman who was playing to give us five familiar hymns. We started in. The Colonel presented the hat to the man immediately on my left. He was sitting on the edge of the platform. He brought out a silver dollar, called a "wheel" in the language of the camp. The second and third men to whom the hat was passed followed the example of the first, each giving a dollar; but the fourth man seemed nervous, and hesitated while he fumbled in his pocket. After considerable delay he brought out a quarter.

"Oh, put that back. Come, now. Bill," said the Colonel, "The Bishop is not after small game today. White chips don't go here. He wants a wheel out of you. Hurry up."
"But, Colonel," said the man, "I hain't got no wheel; I am busted."
"Oh, what you givin' us?" said the Colonel. "Borrow one from Jack. Jack will loan you one."

I was not supposed to hear this dialogue, but the Colonel evidently took no pains to conceal what was going on. After some little parleying Jack loaned his neighbor a "wheel," and the hat passed on. I can remember the Colonel, when he reached the crowd standing at the door, held out the hat with one hand, while with the other he expostulated with the men. The hymns were being rapidly used up, and at last the Colonel returned to the platform with the hat. His face beamed with satisfaction.

After the service I asked him why it took him so long. "Oh," he replied, "Bishop, you see, I charged every feller accordin' to his pile. I know these boys. Most of 'em grub with me. I made one feller cough up a ten-dollar gold piece, and you will find a good many fives in the hat. Let's count it." I need not say that the collection was a generous one.

At four o'clock I went to the hall to help Brother May. As yet no one had come. At length a few women and children and one old man straggled in. Brother May preached on the "Rose of Sharon." It was his maiden effort. The afternoon was very warm, and the perspiration poured forth as my little friend labored with the text. He was thoroughly discouraged, and could not understand why the hall was not full. I ventured to suggest that I feared he had not been very tactful in the morning when he told them that their town was the most "God-forsaken hole" he had ever seen.

I learned afterwards that Brother May remained at the camp only about three weeks. At the end of that time a committee waited on him. The spokesman said:
"Brother May, we understand you don't like our camp."
"No," said Brother May, "It is the worst I ever struck."
"Well, Brother May, would you like to shake off the dust of our camp and leave us for better diggins?"
"You bet I would," was the reply.
"Well, will you leave if we give you seventy-five dollars?"
"Sure I will."
"Will you leave by tomorrow's stage?"
"I certainly will."
"Then here's your money." And Brother May departed to parts unknown.

To return to our Sunday's work. That evening there was another service, and another great crowd. I begged the men to do something towards securing a minister and building a church. I reminded them

*A remote church in Idaho Territory.*
Courtesy of Library of Congress Prints and Photographs Division.

that they had no one to bury their dead, minister to their sick and wounded, baptize their children, administer the holy communion, and preach the Gospel. I told them I would be glad to cooperate with them in any effort they might make. When Monday morning came a committee waited on me with a petition signed by nearly a hundred miners begging me to stay over and give them another talk that night. I consented, and the dance hall was again completely filled. Tuesday morning, just before I took the stage, a committee came to me from a neighboring saloon with a subscription-paper.

One of the committee said: "Now, Bishop, you have been going for us about not having a preacher. Here is a proposition. If you will stay here, and rustle up this preachin' business, and be our Parson, we will stand by you to the tune of two thousand dollars a year. Here it is down in black and white. This is all gilt-edge."

Of course I was surprised and gratified. I replied that, while I felt much complimented by their offer, it was evident they did not understand the nature of my office; that I was a Bishop and had to go from place to place and could stay nowhere long; that I was on my way to the next camp. But I added: "With this liberal offer of two thousand dollars a year I can send you a first-class man."

They hesitated and seemed a little embarrassed. After some consultation one of them said: "Bishop, that was not the deal. The boys subscribed this for you. If you can't come we will have to make a new deal." With that they again disappeared in the saloon.

Returning in a few moments, the spokesman said: "Bishop, here is a new list. If you will send us a first-rate man, a good talker and a good mixer, we will guarantee him at least one thousand dollars a year. Tell him, Bishop, there will be no trouble about money. He shan't be allowed to suffer. We boys will treat him right. Only, please remember," he added, with a twinkle in his eye, "Don't send us no stick."

They had not forgotten Brother May's rebuke, and were not willing to take any chances. The term "good mixer" was new to me then, but I learned that it meant the qualities of good fellowship and sympathy and fraternity. The successful man of God in the mining camps need not lose his dignity or self-respect, but it is of vital importance that he be a man among men, and, above all, possess the capacity of loving men and, with the aid of that gift, know how to reach their hearts.

This is the kind of reception that Talbot received wherever he went. The people were eager and grateful that he came to visit them. Typically when he arrived at a remote camp to preach, the entire population would come to hear him. One recently established settlement was crowded with men, crude buildings and tents, and there were, by actual count, sixty saloons. News of his coming had been posted in advance, and one sign outside a large gambling hall read:

THE BISHOP IS COMING. LET'S ALL TURN OUT TO HEAR THE BISHOP. SERVICE IN GEORGE AND HUMAN'S HALL TOMORROW, SUNDAY, 11 AM AND 8 PM. PLEASE LEAVE YOUR GUNS WITH THE USHER.

During his decade-long ministry in the mountains, Ethelbert Talbot founded three schools: St. Margaret's School in Boise, Idaho, for the education of girls, a Christian school for Indian girls, and St. Matthew's Hall for boys at Laramie, Wyoming. In addition, he established the Frances Holland Hospital at Wallace, Idaho. Talbot took an active interest in the operation of all the churches, and was in touch with the current social and political issues of the area. The people of Idaho, regardless of their religious affiliation, always regarded Ethelbert Talbot as "Our Bishop."

# Approaching the End of an Era

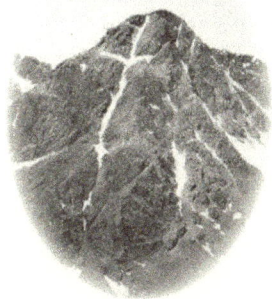

Over and over again we have seen the progression of settlement in the mountain mining regions. As late as 1890, Ethelbert Talbot could recount the same sequence of events that had characterized the earliest camps:

> A big find of gold or silver soon becomes known in a mining country. When the fact is well established, men of all sorts and conditions begin to pour in. Thither go the prospectors—men who have for years been seeking a fortune, generally unsuccessful, but occasionally cheered and urged on by a great strike made by some fortunate comrade. These prospectors are often "grub-staked" with provisions by some backer with money who, in the event of good luck, is to share equally the profits. Thither goes the tin-horn gambler, who prospers with the prosperity of the rest, often amassing a large pile, only to lose it again by an adverse turn of the wheel. Thither always goes the saloon-keeper with his dance hall, assured that if the camp produces anything he will get the lion's share. Later, if the yield is large and promising, the merchants follow. Then the printing press. Last of all, the church enters the field, to be of what service it can in ministering for good to the motley and eager throng. When I went to Idaho the whole section was a dense, uninhabited forest. A few months later a narrow gauge railroad pierced through the woods.

When the twentieth century approached, many of the established mining regions began to fade into history. As Talbot put it, "The average lifetime of a mining camp is brief, and rarely do we find that nature has made such large deposits of the precious metal in any one region." Production would diminish over time, and some were saying that there were no longer any big discoveries to be made in the Rocky Mountains.

One high valley in Colorado had already been prospected and passed over as worthless. It had experienced an earlier gold hoax when unscrupulous promoters "salted" a hole in the ground with gold from another area. But in October 1890 a ranch hand named Bob Womack discovered rich gold ore at Cripple Creek, sparking the last great gold rush in Colorado. The typical "boom" cycle repeated itself, and within three years the area's population would grow to over 10,000 people. Playing their legitimate part in the progression of settlement, home missionaries flocked to the high mountains once again.

In the winter of 1892 Congregationalist minister Horace Sanderson traveled to Cripple Creek, having previously shipped a large tent, a pump organ, chairs, lamps, and song books. Upon his arrival he found that the saloons and gambling halls were already well-established. He quickly arranged to hold his first preaching service in a newly-constructed mercantile store. Here he describes his first experiences in the rough mining community:

> There were no stoves in the camp, and the heating problem was solved by piling up a foot of gravel on the floor, building the fire upon it, and covering the whole with a tin barrel furnished with a smoke pipe. Two preaching services and two Sunday schools were held on the first day, and ninety out of a population of a few hundred attended. During the week lots were contracted for and lumber was bought to build the frame for the large tent. Over this frame the canvas was drawn, the sides and ends were boarded up, and the name "Whosoever Will" painted over the entrance. On the second Sunday services were held in another store, and one hundred forty-one were present, ninety percent of them men. They loved to sing and they sang. The sound rolled out over the camp, and made almost needless the metal triangle which served as a church bell. They listened also and approved. "Don't apologize for the truth, pardner," said one rough miner. "Give it to us straight."

> Families began to come in, and there was no day school for the children. The Superintendent offered the tent for a schoolhouse if the people would pay for a teacher, and he rashly promised to saw the wood. The school attendance the first day was about twenty, and one

*The "Whosoever Will" tent of Congregationalist missionary
Horace Sanderson in Cripple Creek, Colorado, 1893.*
Courtesy of Denver Public Library Western History Collection: X-854.

entry in the missionary's diary for the day reads, "Sawed wood five hours." The tent was opened every afternoon and evening as a free reading room and a place for the men to write letters...The present pastor preaches on the street three or four times a week, gathering an audience of five hundred men in a few minutes. It was thus that the church at Cripple Creek began its career.

As the era of excitement in the mountain mining camps was drawing to a close, the West was being settled by farm and ranch families who were eager to own property and make a better life for themselves. Even though it had been several decades since the first pioneer families came to the Great Plains, the living conditions afterward were just as primitive—possibly even more severe because of a series of drought years on the western ranges.

In 1890 the Episcopal church ordained for ministry a young man named Cyrus Brady. He had been a cadet-midshipman in the US Navy, as well as an official with the railroad. Although he came from a Presbyterian home, his friendship with an Episcopal dean led him to study for the ministry in that denomination. He was assigned to travel a circuit between the distant farming communities on the prairies in Oklahoma and Texas. Here he describes his first experience in one western cow town:

> The town consists of one long, straggling street, lined on both sides with frame stores, saloons, gambling dens, mostly unpainted. There are twelve saloons on the street and only about three hundred people

*Episcopal Minister Cyrus T. Brady*

in the town. Faro, keno, craps, and every other kind of gambling games are going on at full blast and with no attempt at concealment. There every man you meet carries a 45-caliber revolver and a belt of cartridges at his waist. I stayed at the Grand Central. The magnificence of the name and the comforts of the hotel are in an inverse ratio to each other. The rooms are tiny, and the partitions thin boards or canvas screens, therefore the conversations are audible and forcible. I asked for toast last night at supper, and had the pleasure of hearing the cook inquire, "What in ___ does the ___ dude preacher want toast at night for? Tell him he can't have it. I ain't givin' out no toast to nobody at this hour."

There is not a tree in the town, and no grass. The streets are as hard as iron, and it has not rained for months. Water, however, does not appear to be in demand. Very few drink it, and not many wash. The day before I arrived, three desperados broke out of the jail after killing a guard, armed themselves, and fled. The sheriff and a posse made up of all the male citizens, and a few of the female, immediately started in pursuit, overtook them, fought them, killed two of them, and wounded another desperately. One of the deputy sheriffs had his arm blown off in the fight. This was looked upon as quite an ordinary affair, exciting little comment and only a brief notice in the weekly newspaper.

The church is an unceiled, unsheathed, wooden building, unpainted also, the only church in town. Nearly everybody comes to church services. They look upon it as an intellectual diversion, and as a relief from the monotony of faro, at which they always lose. This did not seem a very promising field for the church, yet we subsequently succeeded in establishing services, and now the mission is thriving and the character of the town is entirely changed. I always told the people to have as many services as they liked—that I would conduct them and preach at all of them. As many of them only had services when I would come once every six weeks or so, they sometimes astonished me by the number of occasions for preaching and services that were invented.

Even though the summers had very little rain, an occasional cloudburst could produce dangerous flash floods. Here Brady describes his adventure crossing a raging torrent to get to a wedding on time:

One summer afternoon I found myself twenty-seven miles away from a town down in Indian Territory. I was due there in the evening for services and a wedding. When I went down to the station in the afternoon to take the train, I found that heavy rains and a cloudburst had washed out the bridges, and that no train would be sent through until the next day. For the same reason it would be impossible to drive, so I determined to ride.

A friend of mine offered to get a couple of horses and show me the way. So I telegraphed ahead to the anxious bride that I would be there that night—a little late, perhaps, but that I would surely come. I have ridden many broncos, but this was the worst I ever rode. To be strictly accurate, I could hardly say that I rode him at all. I managed to stick on, and that was all. He bucked and kicked and bit and shied and stopped and balked and did everything for which his breed is famous. It sometimes seemed to me that he was doing all these things at the same time.

When he made up his mind to go, however, he went like the wind. I soon learned that the cowboy method of letting the reins hang loosely, lifting them high in the air, digging in the spurs, and yelling frantically in his ear was the best way to accelerate his pace. He would run and continue to run like a frightened deer as long as the notion seized him. It was exhilarating but dangerous, for the ground was full of prairie dog holes hidden in the buffalo grass, and we never knew when the bronco might put his foot in one, break his leg, and perhaps kill his rider, to say nothing of the dog.

My friend's horse was quite as bad as mine. He said he had meant to give me the better of the two, but mine seemed the worse—perhaps because I rode him. They had strapped on my boots a pair of Mexican spurs with rowels like shark's teeth, which annoyed me very much more than they did my bronco. Every time I inadvertently touched him he had a fit. However, they were the only things by which he could be coerced in any degree.

We had to swim two rivers and one creek. I had crossed them a few days before on the train when they were almost dry in their beds, but now they were roaring torrents. This is a common occurrence with those streams. We forced the horses in the swirling, muddy water of the river, and when we got into the deep water slipped out of the saddle, and retaining tight hold of the high horn, swam alongside to relieve them of our weight. The current swept us down the stream with fearful velocity, and it was only after a long, hard struggle that we reached the other bank a long distance below our starting point.

Late in the evening we reached the town. Pretty much the whole population were out on the sidewalks, including the groom and friends of the bride, and amid wild cheering and laughter, the two bedraggled figures rode down the main street, both horses reserving this particular moment for the final exhibition of their general wickedness. I could just manage to walk to the church that evening, for I was never so sore and stiff in my life. We had a pretty wedding, though the converted saloon was only decorated with tumbleweed, and the carpet upon which the bride walked to the groom's wagon was of the kind popularly known as "rag." The bride was pretty and the groom was manly, and those are the only things which count.

Itinerant preachers of all stripes seemed to live by the following code: "Never miss a preaching appointment." In order to make the rounds, Brady and the other traveling ministers of that day would try to use the fastest available transportation. When they could, they would take the train. Failing that, they would hire a buggy and team. Apart from that, they would ride a bronco. As a last resort, they would use the slowest but often the most reliable transportation: their own two feet.

Being a former railroad man, Brady enjoyed riding the train. It was fast and typically reliable, but even the "iron horse" could break down. Here Brady tells about a time when he was able to use his mechanical skills to help the crew get the train running again:

One day on the Frisco railroad the engine broke down. It was a freight train, and I was the only passenger. Consequently I went out and worked with the train crew, pulling and heaving and hauling with the rest. I knew something about the principles of mechanics, and was familiar with the machine as well, being quite capable of running the engine myself, and was therefore able to advise them to some purpose. The work was carried on under a vigorous and uninterrupted flow of profanity. It was not so shocking as it might be under other circumstances, for I knew the men meant nothing by it—that it was only a matter of habit with them, as it is with ninety people out of a hundred who are guilty of the same bad practice. Finally I suggested an interruption in the swearing, as I was a preacher.

The head brakeman dropped his crowbar with a look of abject astonishment. Everybody else let go at the same time, and the engine settled down again. They looked at me in consternation, which was very amusing. "H__l and blazes!" said the conductor, "You are a what?" "A preacher," I replied. "Well, I'm d___ed!" he answered with a long whistle of astonishment. He regarded me thoughtfully for a moment and finally said, "Well, sir, you work like a man, anyway. Ketch hold again." "All right," I answered, smiling at his frankness, "But no more swearing on this trip." And the promise was kept.

At the close of our maneuvers, when we all stood panting but successful, the engineer remarked: "Well, it's the first time I ever saw a preacher that knowed a reversing lever from a box car before. Come up and ride with me the rest of the way." I found him a pleasant and interesting companion, and whenever I made the town at the end of his run, he never failed to come to church.

Brady had a large territory to cover, and he made his circuit no matter what the weather. The winter season could be especially treacherous. Here he describes one cold Sunday afternoon when he started toward his next appointment after church services in a remote village:

The road lay due south, down a valley through which the wind drove with terrific force. A light snow was beginning to fall as we started out, much against the wise counsels of everybody, but I was young and foolish and did not take heed. We two men were tucked into the sleigh, and between us was a little schoolmistress who had to go to the next town to see a very sick mother. Going down with the wind and snow on our backs was not so bad, and we reached the church at the usual hour.

Two or three men had braved the storm on the chance that I might come, as I had never failed, though they did not expect me. So in the intensely cold church, which it was impossible to heat, with all our winter wrappings on, we knelt down and said the Litany together. Then we got a bite to eat, and the horses having been baited and rubbed down, we started again in spite of the remonstrances of our friends. It was foolish pride, perhaps, but I determined not to miss a single service of that day, if possible. Facing the storm, which had risen and was in the height of its fury, was simply awful. Had I not been one of the more robust of men, I hardly see how I could have survived the exposure of that day. My companion gave up and sank down in the sleigh under the buffalo robes, where I continuously kicked him to keep him from going to sleep.

I had a scarf wrapped around my face, covering it all except the leeward eye, out of which I was continually obliged to brush the frozen snow. My breath froze on the wool, and I thrust my handkerchief between the scarf and my face until the handkerchief froze as well. Then I thought of a little prayer book which I carried in my breast pocket. I opened it in the middle and laid it across my nose under the scarf, making a little roof through which I could breathe.

I tried to keep the way by watching the telegraph poles, but very soon lost sight of them in the whirling snow. The reins lay loose in my benumbed hands. The faithful broncos, however, left to their own devices, toiled slowly along in the face of the blinding drive of the freezing snow over the prairie. I think I had sense enough to keep the horses' heads to the storm, but that was all, and I was too cold and too numb to remember anything. It was dark by this time, and finally the horses stopped at their stable doors. The stablemen were greatly surprised to see us, as they never dreamed we would attempt the journey. It was foolish, of course, but somehow it is the only act of folly in my life upon which I look back with pleasure. Ours was the only church in town that night to have services. Of course the newspapers were full of it, and the next time I had services what a congregation greeted me.

Families on the prairies were very eager to receive visitors, and it was a special event whenever someone came to call. One woman who grew up on the plains of northeastern New Mexico recalled as a young girl that seeing a visitor was "the most precious thing in the world!" This was a common sentiment, especially during the winter season or when holidays rolled around. Here Cyrus Brady describes one Christmas he spent with a poor isolated family in a small prairie settlement:

One Christmas I drove to a little country church where there had never been a Christmas service. The church was a little old brick building right out on the prairie. There was a smoldering fire in a miserable, worn-out stove which hardly raised the temperature of the room a degree, although it filled the place with smoke. The wind had free entrance through the ill-fitting window and door frames, and a little pile of snow formed on the altar during the service. I think there were twelve people who had braved the fury of the storm. There was not an evergreen within a hundred miles of the place, and the only decoration was sage brush. I conducted the service in a buffalo overcoat and a fur cap and gloves, as I have often done. It was short, and the sermon was shorter.

After service I went to dinner at the nearest farm house. There was no turkey, and they did not even have a chicken. The menu was cornbread, ham, and potatoes, and few potatoes at that. There were two children in the family, a girl of six and a boy of five. They were glad to get the ham, since their usual fare was composed of potatoes and cornbread, and sometimes cornbread alone. I had a lunch with me in which there was a small mince pie turnover, and a small box of candy was in my bag. I produced the turnover, which by common consent was divided between the astonished children. "This pie makes it seem like Christmas after all," said the little girl. "Yes," said the boy, "that and the ham." "We didn't have any Christmas this year," continued the girl. "Last year mother made us some potato men. "But this year," interrupted the boy, "potatoes are so scarce that we couldn't have 'em. Mother says that next year perhaps we will have some real Christmas."

They were so brave about it that my heart went out to them. I ransacked my brain, and finally something occurred to me. After dinner I excused myself and hurried back to the church. There were two baskets there which were used for the collection—old, but rather pretty. I selected the best one, and fortunately I had a sewing kit with a pair of scissors, a thimble, needles, thread, a little pin cushion, buttons, etc. I emptied the contents into the collection basket and garnished the dull thing with the ribbon ties from the sewing kit. Returning to the house, I gave the boy my pen knife, which happened to be nearly new, and to the girl the church basket with the sewing things for a work basket. The joy of those children was one of the finest things I have ever witnessed. They were the cheapest and most effective Christmas presents it was ever my pleasure to bestow.

There were times, even when riding the railroad, that winter weather could derail one's holiday plans. It was during the Christmas season when another memorable incident occurred during a snowstorm, which Brady recounts here:

Another Christmas I was snow-bound on one of the obscure branches of a Western railroad. It was snowing hard outside. Our progress had become slower and slower. Finally, in a deep cut, we stopped. There were three men, one woman, and two little children in the car—no other passengers in the train. One of the trainmen started on a lonely and somewhat dangerous tramp of several miles up the road to the next station to call for the snow plow, and the rest of us

*Workmen clearing snow that drifted above the tracks during a winter storm.*
Courtesy of Denver Public Library Western History Collection: GB-8148

settled down to spend the night. Certainly we could not hope to be extricated before the next evening, especially as the storm then gave no signs of abating.

We all went up to the front of the car and sat around by the stove, in which we kept up a bright fire, and in such circumstances we speedily got acquainted with each other. One of the men was a "drummer," a traveling salesman for a notion house; another was a cowboy; the third was a big cattleman; and I was the last. We soon found that the woman was a widow who had maintained herself and the children precariously, since the death of her husband, by sewing and other odd jobs, but had at last given up and was going back to live with her mother, also a widow, who had some property.

The poor little threadbare children had cherished anticipations of a joyous Christmas with their grandmother. From their talk we could hear that a Christmas tree had been promised them, and all sorts of things. They were intensely disappointed at the blockade. They cried and would not be comforted. Fortunately the woman had a great basket filled with substantial provisions, which, by the way, she generously shared with the rest of us, so we were none of us hungry.

As night fell, we tipped up two of the seats, and with our overcoats made two good beds for the little folks. Just before they went to sleep, the drummer said to me: "Say, Parson, we've got to give those children some Christmas!" "That's right," said the cowboy. "I'm agreed," added the cattleman. "Madam," said the drummer, addressing the woman with the easy assurance of his class, after a brief consultation between us, "We are going to give your kids some Christmas." The woman beamed at him gratefully.

"Yes, children," said the now enthused drummer, as he turned to the open-mouthed children, "Santa Claus is coming 'round tonight for sure. We want you to hang up your stockings." "We ain't got none," quivered the little girl, "'ceptin' those we've got on, and ma says it's too cold to take 'em off." "I've got two new pair of woolen socks," said the cattleman eagerly, "which I ain't never wore, and you are welcome to 'em." There was a clapping of little hands, and then the two faces fell as the oldest remarked: "But Santa Claus will know they are not our stockings, and he will fill them with things for you instead."

"Lord love you," said the burly cattleman, roaring with laughter, "He won't bring me nothin'. One of us will sit up, anyway, and tell him it's for you. You've got to hustle to bed right away, because he may be here any time now." Then came one of those spectacles which we sometimes meet once or twice in a lifetime. The children knelt down on the rough floor of the car beside their improvised beds. Instinctively, the hands of the men went to their heads and at the first words of "Now I lay me down to sleep," four hats came off. The cowboy stood twirling his hat and looking at the little kneeling figures. The cattleman's vision seemed dimmed, while in the eyes of the traveling man there shone a distant look.

The children were soon asleep, and the rest of us engaged in earnest conversation. What should we give them? was the question. "It don't seem to me that I've got anything to give 'em," said the cowboy mournfully. "I'm in much the same fix," said the cattleman. "Never mind, boys," said the drummer. "You all come along with me to the baggage car." So off we trooped. He opened his trunks and spread before us such a glittering array of trash and trinkets as almost took away our breath. "There," he said, "look at that. We'll just pick out the best things from the lot, and I'll donate them all."

"No, you don't," said the cowboy. "I'm goin' to buy what I want and pay fer 'em too." "That's my judgment too," said the cattleman. "I think that will be fair," I said. "The traveling man can donate what he pleases, and we can each of us buy what we please." I think we spent hours looking over the stock which the obliging man spread out all over the car for us. The trainman caught the infection, too, and all hands finally went back to the coach with such a load of stuff as you never saw before. We filled the socks, and two seats besides. The grateful mother was simply dazed.

As we all stood about, gleefully surveying our handiwork, including the bulging socks, the engineer remarked: "We've got to get some kind of a Christmas tree." So two of us plowed off on the prairie—it had stopped snowing and was bright moonlight—and wandered around until we found a good-sized piece of sage brush, which we brought back and solemnly installed, and the woman decorated it with bunches of tissue paper. We hung train lanterns around it.

We were so excited that we actually could not sleep. The contagion of the season was strong upon us, and I know not which were the more delighted the next morning, the children or the amateur Santa Clauses. Those children never did have, and probably never will have, such a Christmas again. And to see the thin face of that mother flush with unusual color when we handed her one of those monstrous red plush albums which we had purchased jointly and in which we had all written our names in lieu of our photographs, and between the leaves of which the cattleman had generously slipped a hundred-dollar bill, was worth being blockaded for a dozen Christmases.

During the morning we had a little service in the car, and I am sure no more heartfelt body of worshipers ever poured forth their thanks for the Incarnation than those men, that woman, and the little children. "It feels just like church," said the cowboy gravely to the cattleman. The trainman who had gone to headquarters returned with the snow plow early in the afternoon, but what was more to the purpose, he brought a whole cooked turkey with him, so the children had turkey, a Christmas tree, and presents to their heart's content.

After Brady had been ministering on the prairies for three years he tallied the miles he had covered. He found that he traveled over ninety-one thousand miles by railroad, wagon, and horseback. He had given over a thousand sermons, as well as making personal calls, performing marriages and baptisms, and doing all of the other tasks that were required of him in the remote parts of the West.

The age of the automobile was born in 1886 when German engineer Carl Benz introduced his *Patent-Motorwagon*. Within a few short years after the turn of the twentieth century, the Ford Model-T became popular all across America. The proliferation of the automobile would mark the end of an era for the itinerant preacher. As Ferenc Szasz put it,

"The automobile permanently altered the religious history of the Great Plains." People could drive long distances in relatively short periods of time, and they no longer needed the preachers to visit them. Since the bigger cities seemed "closer" now, the farmers and ranchers began to attend the larger and more popular churches. The age of the itinerant preacher was coming to an end.

# Reflections on the Pioneer Preachers

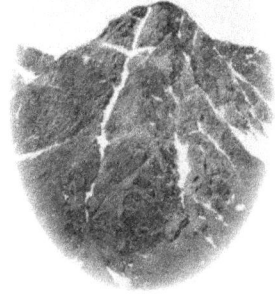

In 1899, at the age of eighty-seven and just two years before his death, John L. Dyer of Colorado took the train from his home in Denver to hold preaching services in Breckenridge. By this time he was no longer able to get around well, and he used crutches in order to walk even short distances. The local newspaper reported,

> Rev. Father Dyer made one of his itinerant preaching tours during the week to some of the mining towns. The reverend gentleman bears his many years well in spite of the accident a few years ago which compels him to get around on crutches. He has known and visited Breckenridge for thirty-seven years. He left here on Tuesday for Kokomo.

What this newspaper account did not report was that Kokomo was over twenty-five miles away, and to get there Dyer would have to cross the Continental Divide at Hoosier Pass (11,542 feet), as well as probably crossing the Mosquito Range over his old route through Mosquito Pass (13,185 feet). By this time the Methodist Church already had many preachers stationed throughout the area, so Dyer's trip was something he determined to do on his own. After crossing Hoosier Pass, Dyer descended into South Park where he happened to meet the presiding elder of this district on an old logging road. The man was shocked to see Father Dyer hobbling along on his crutches, and he asked Dyer what he was doing there. Dyer replied, "I thought there might be some people over here who needed preaching."

What could have compelled the elderly preacher to make such a journey in his last days? He could have rested comfortably in a nice home in Denver for the rest of his life, and yet there he was on another rugged trail in his beloved Rocky Mountains. "I thought there might be some people over here who need preaching." This simple statement reveals the heart and soul of a man who had dedicated his life to ministry on the frontier.

Thomas Harwood, John Dyer's friend and protégé in New Mexico, knew this sentiment all too well. He may have had Father Dyer in mind when he later wrote:

> It is a fact of history, which the lives of those who have accomplished most for the cause of Christ in the work of the ministry reveal, that the secret of their success was in their deep and earnest love for souls. Their education was often deficient, their methods of study and their manner of preaching irregular and defective, but their fervor for the salvation of the souls of men counterbalanced all such difficulties and made them effective and useful ministers in a very eminent degree.

> There are those who say that if only the memory were more richly stored, and the logical faculty more thoroughly disciplined, and the art of rhetoric more fully mastered, the cause of Christ in the world would receive a new impulse. I am free to say that I have no sympathy with such views. God forbid that I should in the least underrate education. The more of it the better, but the chief want of the ministry today is not learning, but manifest love—the love that is so unselfish that it measures not its self-sacrifice, but finds supreme delight in greatly multiplying them, that in its deep devotion to the salvation of souls, forgets the thorns, the burdens it has to bear, and the roughness of its own pathway.

How did they manage it? Alexander Darley established ten Presbyterian churches during his five-year ministry in the San Luis Valley of Colorado. His brother George Darley built almost as many in the rugged San Juan Mountains to the west. Thomas Harwood started sixty-six Methodist churches, chapels, and schools in New Mexico. John Spalding established over fifty Episcopal churches in Colorado, while fellow ministers Tuttle and Talbot started dozens of churches and schools in Wyoming, Idaho, and Montana. Sheldon Jackson organized twenty-three Presbyterian churches in Colorado during a single year. Methodist William Van Orsdel started one hundred churches as well as a half dozen hospitals and schools in Montana.

In his assessment of the character of a successful missionary in the West, Cyrus Brady concluded that it required a rare breed of men to minister on the frontier. It took grit, determination, will-power, strength of character, physical endurance, and complete dedication to the work. Brady commented:

> The physical weakling has no place in the missionary work in the West. The distances to be covered are so great, the number of places necessarily allotted to one man so many, the means of transportation so varied and unpleasant, the demands upon strength and bodily vigor so overwhelming, that it is no easy matter for the strongest to live up to the requirements.

There was a time when I attempted to recreate a small portion of one circuit that Thomas Harwood might have traveled in northern New Mexico. I was on foot, as Harwood probably would have been in that particular place. My journey started at the ruins of a log cabin where an Irishman and his wife had raised seven daughters in a remote mountain area. With the exception of the young schoolmistress who boarded with his family, all of his nearest neighbors were many miles away. I was immediately impressed with the stark beauty of that high meadow situated at around 8,000 feet in elevation, nestled between

*The remote log cabin home of Timothy Ring, his wife, and seven daughters in a high mountain meadow of northern New Mexico.*

12,000-foot peaks to the north and south. I remembered Harwood's fascination with the natural world and was struck by the feeling that he probably would have loved this country very much.

A light rain shower cooled the evening air, and before I retired to the relative comfort of my tent I walked some distance from my camp in the darkness. A yellowish moon began to rise, and I was flooded with a wave of sheer loneliness and isolation in this place. The scene had not changed much in the 150 years since Dyer and Harwood tramped these mountains. They slept under the same immense blanket of starry sky as each of them traveled alone through the wilderness. On a night like this the rain would have brought a chill, and it may have been difficult to sleep amid the howling of coyotes on all sides of the valley. It would have taken a man of determination to endure these conditions night after night for forty years of ministry in the mountains.

The next day I hiked up a creek to another high meadow on the southeastern slopes of a 12,000-foot peak. Near the head of the canyon at almost 9,000 feet in elevation were the ruins of a small family homestead. Another Irishman and his wife had raised their six children in this place. As I investigated the tumble-down log cabin, I could not imagine how eight people lived in those small rooms. At one point I turned around to look at the view from what would have been their front door, and I could see why John McCrystal chose that particular location. The vista was breathtaking, with Baldy Mountain in the distance and the immense mountain valley spread out below.

Although the place is beautiful, it is extremely remote. I tried to put myself in Thomas Harwood's shoes—making a ministry call to a large family in an isolated mountain canyon. They would be overjoyed

*Ruins of a residence in the high mountains of northeastern New Mexico.*

to have a visitor. Even though he must have been exhausted from the climb, Harwood's focus would be on the needs of this growing household. How did he maintain the right attitude for Christian service after the literal marathon of traveling to such remote sites?

Leaving the high canyon I ventured southeast into Whiteman Vega, which had been named for the family who made their home there. This was an even more immense mountain valley which stretched for miles in each direction. It was surrounded almost entirely by steep-sided mesas and cliffs, and as I stood among the ruins of the family home I was overwhelmed by the staggering distances on all sides. I felt very small and insignificant in comparison to the vastness and apparent infinity of this place.

At one point along the trail I noticed an unusual arrangement of short stones poking up at regular intervals, and I realized that this was an old graveyard. Most of the headstones were fashioned by hand from local rocks. There were no markings except for crude crosses scraped or chipped into some of the stones. Two of the graves at the far end were outlined in smaller pebbles and raised in elevation from the others, indicating that this may have been a much-loved mother and father who were buried together. I estimated that there were twenty-seven graves in that spot, and I began to wonder who performed the burial services there. My thoughts turned to the necessity for the pastoral care of these people and their families. Who performed the baptisms, christenings, marriages, and funerals? Who taught the truths of the Bible to these isolated mountain people?

Step after step, on and on I walked for hours at a time, often making progress only by willing myself to place one foot in front of the other. A man has lots of time to think during such treks. What would have occupied Thomas Harwood's mind on his journeys? Would he have spent his time in prayer? Would images of his loved ones float through his mind? Did he mentally plan his sermons as he tramped the trails? How did he keep himself from being overwhelmed with homesickness and loneliness?

Ministry in such places would have required a rare combination of what today we might label introversion and extroversion. The introvert would be well-adapted to traveling alone in the wilderness and bearing the sense of utter isolation in the vast stretches of the Rocky Mountain West. The extrovert would have been able to quickly gather a crowd, preach to large groups, counsel and encourage all the individuals who needed help. Ferenc Szasz correctly stated, "The ministers who succeeded best in the West did so largely through the force of personality." But it was a man with a rare type of personality who could be effective as a minister in the Far West.

Around the same time that Father J.L. Dyer was making his final preaching trip from Breckenridge through the Colorado mountains, Episcopal minister Cyrus Brady was writing an eloquent description that could apply equally to Dyer and countless other pioneer preachers:

> The hem of the garment of Progress is dabbled with the blood of men who have made way for her by giving up the treasure of their hearts to facilitate her advance. In that deluge of men which has rolled ever westward over the prairies, crept up the long slopes of the Rocky Mountains, finally beating over them in mighty waves to fall in thunderous surges on the other side—those who have led the way on the crest of the waves have been beaten into human spray, and having so smoothed the path, go by the wayside. The footprints of civilization are those made by the feet of the men who stand upon the wild prairies and high mountaintops of the West and bring the good news.

We owe a tremendous debt of gratitude to men like the preachers whose stories are presented here. At the very least, we must remember them. At the very most, we must strive to be more like them.

# Suggested Reading

Beardsley, Isaac Haight. *Echoes from Peak and Plain*. Cincinnati: Curts & Jennings, 1898.

Brady, Cyrus Townsend. *Recollections of a Missionary in the Great West*. New York: Charles Scribner's Sons, 1900.

Bristol, Sherlock. *The Pioneer Preacher*. New York: Fleming H. Revell, 1887.

Brummitt, Stella W. *Brother Van*. New York: The Missionary Education Movement, 1919.

Clark, Joseph B. *Leavening the Nation: The Story of American Home Missions*. New York: The Baker & Taylor Company, 1903.

Cross, Roselle T. *Notes of Long Service in Colorado: The Home Missionary.* NY: Congregational Home Missionary Society, April, 1896.

Darley, George M. *Pioneering in the San Juan*. New York: Fleming H. Revell Company, 1899.

Davis, Carlyle C. *Olden Times in Colorado*. Los Angeles: Phillips Publishing, 1916.

Dyer, John L. *Snow-Shoe Itinerant*. Cincinnati: Cranston & Stowe, 1890.

Feister, Mark. *Look for Me in Heaven*. Breckenridge: Dyer Methodist Church, 1980.

Goode, William H. *Outposts of Zion*. Cincinnati: Poe & Hitchcock, 1863.

Harwood, Thomas. *History of New Mexico Spanish and English Missions of the Methodist Episcopal Church from 1850 to 1910: Two Volumes*. Albuquerque: El Abogado Press, 1908, 1910.

Hilts, Joseph H. *Experiences of a Backwoods Preacher*. Toronto: Methodist Mission Rooms, 1892.

Jones, T.L. *From the Gold Mine to the Pulpit*. Cincinnati: Jennings & Pye, 1903.

Kellogg, Harriet S. *Life of Mrs. Emily J. Harwood*. Albuquerque: El Abogado Press, 1903.

Kirby, Linda K. *Heritage of Heroes*. Denver: Trinity United Methodist Church, 1988.

Randall, George Maxwell. *Report of the Missionary Bishop of Colorado, New Mexico, and Wyoming*, 1871.

*Rocky Mountain Directory and Colorado Gazetteer for 1871*. Denver: S.S. Wallihan and Company, 1870.

Schoolland, John B. *A Pioneer Church: First Presbyterian Church of Boulder, Colorado Territory*. Boulder: Johnson Publishing Company, 1972.

Stanley, Edwin James. *Life of Rev. L.B. Stateler*. Nashville: Publishing House of the M.E. Church South, 1907.

Stewart, Robert Laird. *Sheldon Jackson: Pathfinder and Prospector of the Missionary Vanguard in the Rocky Mountains and Alaska*. New York: Fleming H. Revell Company, 1908.

Szasz, Ferenc Morton. *The Protestant Clergy in the Great Plains and Mountain West, 1865-1915*. Albuquerque: University of New Mexico Press, 1988.

Talbot, Etherbert. *My People of the Plains*. New York: Harper and Brothers, 1906.

Townsend, John K. *Sporting Excursions in the Rocky Mountains*. London: Henry Colburn, 1840.

Tuttle, Daniel S. *Reminiscences of a Missionary Bishop*. New York: Thomas Whittaker, 1906.

www.ingramcontent.com/pod-product-compliance
Lightning Source LLC
Chambersburg PA
CBHW032047090426
42744CB00004B/112